so fast as Mike Reid, the cockney creator of the pill-happy market suede-head, new in the cast of standard comedy chara extraordinarily accurate regional accents, from Williams's Ba different shades of Liverpool Irish, that spark a solid partisan s as quickly as football colours.

On one of the early programmes there was a comedian who never reappeared. His face was not so much dispassionate in the manner of Dawson, as menacing. His jokes were sour, even vicious — 'Y'know the lad who ran over a Pakistani. Went back to see if he was okay. Fella fillin' in a hole at the side of the road. Says, "What are y' doing?" "I'm buryin' that Pakistani you ran over." "Why, wor he dead?" "Well he said he wasn't but y' know what bloody liars they are."' And they were spat out from a face drawn into the staring, taut, near-bilious expression a drunken man possesses just before he completely loses his temper. He embodied the incredible callousness that lies behind Bill Tidy's best cartoons. How he and Dawson might confront Kenneth Williams, whose literacy, articulation, rambling inventiveness, whose innuendos that 'only you and I' can understand, whose rococo camp, place him as the most extravagant development of the Southern tradition, is something to make an audience tremble.

Kenneth Williams is so refined in his style that he twists like an anachronistic snake among the lumps and bumps that make up the *Carry On* team and the *Carry On* performance. The cast is no longer out of McGill. The cherry noses are blue around the nostrils. The cheery smiles are circumscribed by aching jaws. From Bamforth's of Holmfirth, from Constance's of Littlehampton (who still publish McGill), from Sunny Pedro's of Christ-knows-where come the designs and scenarios that seem more appropriate to the *Carry On* saga. The boss-eyed cock-artists and buxom crumpet of Fitzpatrick and Taylor, the inflatable nymphos of Pedro and Milla and Bob, the unbelievably primitive images of Bashful. McGill was jaunty, saucy, innocent. These dishevelled suitors and tumescent titsellinas have none of the naughty nudging quality of McGill's characters. They are after their oats and the general feeling is not so much one of breezy lads and lassies on holiday, but more that of alcoholic commercial travellers on a perpetual headlong course of lechery. Somewhere between Arthur Ferrier's leggy wartime pin-up drawings and Diana Dors's image as the GI's Surrey Bypass dream, comes this creation of Bob's, who, backing on to the bedknob in her frilly négligé, cries, 'Oh George, I didn't hear you come in!' There she stoops, impaled, with her massive tits, her mammary buttocks, her blonde bang and her legs exactly twice the length of her torso. Along comes Barbara Windsor, all ready to pop her bras, lose her knickers, mince along hotel corridors, tumble out of the wrong bed and into the wrong back seat, with Charles Hawtrey, Frankie Howerd, Sid James, Kenneth

Connor and even Hattie Jacques.

And the breezy breezes lag a little with an odour of the oil-rigs. And the belly-laughs drop down a little too soon into wheezes. There is cancer behind the hacking cough of the libidinous bar-fly, dust on the Babycham glasses, too much cigarette ash in the carpet. The fatigue has stripped away the old, warm, music-hall good nature and left the material bare in its content of weakness, sex and common failings. Through the closing-time haze we can just about make out the figure of a toothless, boozy little man who seems at home with material laid so naked, who seems undisturbed by phlegmy coughs and spilled gin. It isn't Hawtrey but it is Hawtrey's true begetter, for Frank Randle drooled his toothless gums and waggled his varicose knees at successive thousands of helpless, shrieking mill-town wives on Blackpool's South Pier throughout the forties and the early fifties. A sad and sick man in his later private life, Randle could imply, describe and render visible more unqualified filth than any comedian before or since. Much of it was witless to say the least, completely unfunny except in so far as he repeatedly indicated that blowing away of all pretences, that collapse of all taboos which occurs when the shit is found in the kitchen cupboard, when the hapless drunk vomits on the table, when the sewerage overflows. Randle, in fact, was himself a visibly overflowing sewerage system. He never wore his teeth, the better to facilitate the strings of saliva that fell from his jaws every time the appointed chorus girls — 'A couple of hottuns' — bounced their mounds across the stage in provocation. In his ancient waiter sketch, bored stiff at the lack of custom, he hawks mightily from somewhere in his chest, rolls the dredging round his mouth, inflated cheek to inflated cheek, matching each inflation with a manic rolling of his eye at his screaming front row, then lets the lot go, splat, to where it can be seen, sliding lugubriously down the wall. But hark, someone is coming. Randle seizes his napkin and wipes the wall, then, with the same napkin, busies himself polishing glasses before the customers enter.

His bar-room sketch began with an elaborate gastric play with the beer itself. The brew is ordered, drawn and held to the light. 'Heehee,' growls Randle. 'All slops', the esses spraying out from those insatiable gums. He takes a mouthful. The inevitable girl enters, sits on a bar stool and crosses her gartered legs to show delicious acres of thigh and gusset. Randle's jaw drops in sudden violent tumescence. His knees waggle and his larynx gargles enthusiastically as the complete mouthful of beer drops down his pristine shirt front. Circus-clown stuff transformed by the formality of the proscenium. After much dropping of pennies so that the view might surreptitiously be better enjoyed, after much clapping of the right palm against the left bicep, much eye-rolling and yet more knee-waggling on Randle's part, the girl finishes her drink and leaves. Randle recovers himself

sufficiently to belch, which he does with a sound like the tearing of some substantial fabric. After a pause he spits. 'By gum,' he says, 'I miss the owd spittooin.' 'Aye,' says the barman. 'You always did.'

Another mouthful, another belch. He holds his pint to the light. 'By gum,' he burbles, 'there's some burps in this ale.'

Another mouthful.

'By gum, I s'l be glad when I've 'ad enough.' He spits again. Girl walks on and off again. More fitful drooling.

'I say,' he says. 'You've to be careful in this 'ere pub. I were in t'other day and I wanted to go to — tha knows — to the—.' He waggles his backside, scratches his balls and the whole theatre explodes with women who shriek as though they had been suddenly fingered. 'So before I went I stuck a notice on me ale sayin', "I 'Ave Spit In This Ale." When I came back someone 'ad written underneath, "So 'Ave I."'

Another shriek.

'But I supped it just t' same. . . .'

And so it goes on. Randle at his best played an old old man. The combination of billy-goat randiness and drooling senility was his special area. His accent was thick with the rich 'R' of the Lancashire Pennines and there was a good deal of the farmyard, the midden, of nostalgic rustic excesses, about his role. You could come away from a Randle performance physically crippled with sheer exhaustion from having laughed so much, and with each ache in the gut and the side came the exquisite relief that we were all of us, in that smoky noisy theatre, mere alimentary systems, mere overgrown infants, mere flesh and blood, that we were thus rendered, by the discovery, just for a short hour or two, one flesh and one soul, so where could harm ever be? Who or what could ever threaten or conquer our common clay?

# Greetings from Blackpool

THE TOWER BALLROOM

THE TOWER.

The British are a literate people. In terms of visual perception it would not be true to say they were undeveloped. Rather they have been overwhelmed with the printed and the written word. TV has extended the media for the dissemination of information but has failed to have any obvious effect on the buildings and houses of which our cities are composed. A visit to a Fun Fair such as Blackpool reveals a conglomeration of disparate parts, a jumble of unrelated bits, forcibly welded together but in uneasy and unharmonious squalor. Each part must be focused upon, each section examined in isolation. There are no perspectives, no overall merging into an iconic whole. The result is turbulence, a seething discomfort. It is only when information is displayed in printed form that the jumble comes together and imparts meaning. Lack of information implies emptiness, a void inviting boredom. Every surface is agitated and filled up with incident. All is imitative, bearing the appearance of the super-real world. Given an Identity. A track support becomes a comic-book Gulliver, identified by the conventional signs of that jolly giganticism associated with W. Disney rather than J. Swift. Nightfall throws a merciful obscurity over all, the electric lights that had dangled like plastic fruit in sagging lines shine out in new delineations, the same hackneyed images of comic-book drawing rather than cinema, barely alluding to them, relying on a compact of experience.

Somewhere between the unabashed randiness of the mill-girl on holiday and the stony-eyed stoicism of the Methodist mother-of-ten there is an area of sexual wryness, of sore flesh, of easily inflamed disappointment, of savagely interknotted double standards where a particular eroticism is to be enjoyed. Robust but not bucolic. Perverse but not effete. Angry but not destructive.

Its character as the collision point of numerous passionately supported opposites provides its further definition. Sadistic and humanitarian. Puritanical and hedonistic. Crude, with imperceptible taboos. You may openly hand round pornography in mixed company but you must never ever say fuck. The only people who are allowed to say fuck in mixed company are queers and prostitutes who are commonly held to have forfeited the security of family structure and are therefore excused the taboos whose purpose is to hold the family structure in place. Homosexuality is warmly tolerated in queer pubs, drag clubs, in the forces, in London, but seldom at work or within the neighbourhood. It is tolerated where the whole crowd is pretending not to be married; public places where taboos can go to the winds, far from home, not too near the family.

So whilst there is a clinging to that straight, functional act whereby the firstborn is got and the rings exchanged and the investments made in houses, cars, layettes and front-room suites, there is always a hunger for the lost world of teenage encounters. Stage Three longs for Stage Two. The woman who has been decent all her married life is anxious to make it clear either with a twinkle in her eye or a sudden shriek of confessional laughter that this was not always the case. She stays pretty close to her husband anyway, and he to her, because they recognise in one another the pining for the fucks they never had, for besides the nostalgia that sells the jet-black hair-dye and the pancake make-up is the curiosity and hunger for the privilege and licence enjoyed by those with either money, education or sophistication enough to be unimpeded by an inherited Protestant ethic and unwanted children. Veritably the orgasmic envy and desire for public-scandal figures like Christine Keeler or Mick Jagger can only be sublimated by the most aggressively expressed hatred and condemnation. Those granite crosses from the Pennine chapels where Wesleyanism first grew its English roots have kept us out of the orgy so long what can we do but seize them as cudgels to revenge ourselves on those who have avoided any of our difficulties, against the gypsies and tarts who remain at Stage Two, against the drug-taking intellectuals at Stages Six and Seven with their divorces and their birth control, against idle West Indians and Roman Catholic Irishmen and wogs? This very anger is an erotic power significantly greater than anything Christine Keeler is ever likely to have enjoyed. At its best it is the driving force of *Wuthering Heights*. At its not-too-distant worst it is the driving force of the English sexual murderer. Somewhere between it is the curious and distorted passion existing between the couple at the P. J. Proby performance. Proby, some years past his prime when his mighty phallus split the fabric of his jeans on at least one celebrated occasion, is now reduced to touring on the working men's club circuit. At the peak of his performance a female adorer, now married and in her late twenties, tears off her knickers (supermarket floral) amidst shrieks of encouragement from her friends, rushes down front and hurls them on the stage. Her husband, who would have applauded had anyone else's wife done this, crashes his glass to the table, leaps after her and smashes his craggy knuckles into her face. Pandemonium. Shrieks of abuse, encouragement, restraint. Wise nods of masculine approval. Tears. While Proby continues to hammer out his somewhat devitalised rock-and-roll from the stage. And after that the post-orgasmic quietude. The muttering groups outside. The palmed cigarettes and the delicious smouldering itch of sexual hatred.

Rituals of this kind happen far too frequently to be accidental. There is something there that demands to concoct this melting pot of multiple standards, then bring it repeatedly to the boil. Proby, who is hired as nothing else but a sexual stimulant, is presented at a venue within the neighbourhood, t'Club, where home is too close for taboos to be relaxed, where good neighbours watch one another, sitting in family groups, wrapped in their best clothes, pretending to have reached Stage Five, their older folk, many of whom have reached Stage Five, simpering over their Tia Maria. The mutually alienating elements have been brought compulsively together. This is no social disaster. This is an aphrodisiac of the most profound and violent kind. It is sex, which is most profoundly threatened, defending itself by scratching its own sores. The real emasculator is not chapel, nor priest, nor ignorance, nor unwanted children, although all these contribute. The real emasculator is hard work. Therefore sex forfeits the relaxed, moon-kissed lyrical mood it maintains for the leisured class and finds for itself an iconography that will express the fantastic intensity that builds up when the spirit is desperate and the flesh is exhausted.

Between Proby's stuffed trousers and the good wife's elastic-bound body there is the iconography of repression eroticised as compression. Mother's slack mounds crammed into pantee-girdles, Proby's notorious prick straining at that Carnaby Street velveteen. And thence to elastic swimming costumes, uplift brassieres, suspender belts, suspenders over huge buttocks, drainpipe trousers, black shiny stockings, buckle-top boots, low-cut blouses pulled tight over enlarged breasts and tucked severely into three-inch patent leather belts, desperate half-erections swaddled like the Christ child in transparent latex, swollen limbs in elastic stockings, hernias in their belts and trappings emulated in jock-straps and cricket boxes, the odd clenched paraphernalia of the Soho surgical stores, finally tight foreskins.

The icon, then, of either sex is a penis. A perpetual erection that never comes, a symbol finally for that tumultuous sexual urge that never, through one reason and another but mainly through sheer fatigue, is ever completely consummated. It is survival culture again. The difficulty is dealt with by being itself transformed into eros.

Behind this is a formidable physicality. There is no effete languishing over the lissom young with Nabokov, or after the avuncular old with Sagan. There is a wish to maintain that formal cuirass which probably first appeared in the publicity for body-building clubs and soon invaded the matrist world of the post-Sarah Bernhardt, principal-boy sex-symbol, to produce the woman of the hard, upturned nipple, the high-gloss lipstick and the racehorse thigh, and the man of the massive shoulders, the gigolo's hips and the well-packed cod-piece. The prototypes had reached full perfection by the mid-forties and were tied up with the public images of certain film stars and singers. Amongst men the aesthetic pumped new life and muscle, and indeed volume, into twenties heart-throbs, grew clearer with the emerging images of Douglas Fairbanks and Clark Gable, became then Robert Mitchum, Kirk Douglas, Victor Mature, Johnny Weissmuller and Rock Hudson, who were all the nearest Hollywood could manage to the comic-book supermen who had sprung up in the late thirties, Captain Marvel, Flash Gordon and even Clark Kent himself, all of them space-age versions of Tarzan whose streamlined figure, drawn first by Harold Foster and then by Hogarth, was a powerful prototype; thence to Brando, Presley, ultimately Tom Jones and the ageing Proby. It is significant that when the female fashion moved on through Marilyn Monroe to Brigitte Bardot and the male image moved through James Dean toward Jagger and Hendrix, the Northern working class, hearing in the distance that dying fall, that *thanatos* in the music that comes with art and taste, put on the brakes and continued to idolise figures in whom heterosexual polarity was most strongly marked; figures like Tom Jones and Diana Dors.

Amongst the female ideals the saucy flappers and their thirties followers, the holiday pick-ups of McGill's postcards (who incidentally remained stuck in the early thirties even though McGill drew them well into the forties) also suffered inflation, filled-out sweaters with Lana Turner, bathing suits with Esther Williams, evening gowns with Rita Hayworth and the Goldwyn Girls, and anything at all with Jayne Mansfield, Diana Dors and Sabrina. The music for this prototype was filtered off from jazz and presented in the husky confessionals of Dorothy Squires.

There was a world of the British blonde bombshell that was a world of bypass roadhouses and market towns where GIs from the nearby base passed their lazy evenings over a beer by the jukebox. The leggy lady opportunists ordered spectacu-lar Pimms No. 1 so that they could nuzzle their Pekinese noses into miniature oriental gardens afloat on alcohol, and later, after the final conscious scotch, cars as big as midnight winds swept down roads that were built for donkey carts and hysterical rustic lips attempted Brooklyn accents.

A Hollywood dreamworld grotesquely reconstructed, with the GIs as voluntary extras, whilst the English working class merged their dream of sophistication with their dream of sexual freedom, so that not only did Dicky Valentine, and indeed any other popular singer up to the Beatles, have to develop an American accent, but you could hear the mid-Atlantic tone creeping in when girls were first approached at the Palais, when girls were finally submitting on the back seat of the car, no doubt when girls were being consoled on many a disillusioned wedding night.

Until recently, when pubic hair has made its way into the cheaper pin-up magazines, straight pornography had little part in this elaborate erotic structure. The old Windmill Theatre eroticism, which is very close to that working-class eroticism built on taboo, capitulated some years ago to the greater extravagances of the Paul Raymond empire. Nevertheless Raymond's greater frankness and far more highly developed camp were slow to catch on in the Northern cities. The frisson is lost if the light is too bright and those hairy labia and straining members can be clearly seen. Unlike the facts of dirt and work and the arsehole, the genital truths had to be retained as a fulcrum of tensions and therefore could not wholly be admitted or even realised. The repression had to be preserved so that the itch of compression could continue to be celebrated. Any working men's club performer knows that you can say shit but you can never say fuck, or cunt, or prick. Paul Raymond knows what you have to do to a London act before it will go down in the very funky new clubs in Manchester. You have to clean it up, or you have to coarsen it.

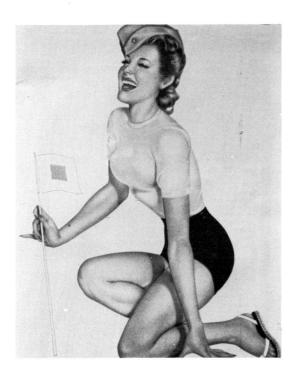

So the home is preserved. Those gross mounds with their big brown nipples must be crammed into cups of wire, elastic and stretched nylon. Those over-productive vaginas must be pursed in their own lips and bound shut with panels and seams and groins of formidable strength. The minute the breast falls free and the perm is washed out so that Primavera tresses cascade untrammelled across femininity graced by air and light, is the moment that specially frustrated erection is sacrificed to something different.

Consequently, flowing muslins and exquisite transparencies are refused or held suspect each time they come into fashion, as were the first bikinis, ginghams, see-throughs, any form or material that indicated that some relaxed correlation could be established between the genitals and the revealing light of day. The complete denuding of pornography, particularly in the current five-colour glossy post-*Penthouse* mode, has only recently ceased to be a joke and a curiosity, has only begun to erode those circling rituals of pride and elaborate tension.

Consequently, masturbator's magazines have strayed from the convention and have taken on a middle-class devitalised quality. Bikinis must be tight or wet or made of some material which exaggerates the restrictive, confining creases. For years nudity and pubic hair, when they appeared, had to be flatly lit and gauchely posed. *Parade*, by no means a middle-class periodical, features a big proportion of sun-and-surf nudes and was the first cheap mag to move on to pubic hair. The girls were, however, not snapped in their natural female nakedness. The myth was neither that of the jet-set nymphet disconsolate on the private beach, nor that of the intelligent woman striding blithely into the inheritance of her own shameless orgasm. The girls were set for the cameras like any burlesque performer: heads back, eyes lidded; chests out, stomachs in. The myth was the old paraphernalia of coyness, the ancient peek-a-boo masks that retain the privileges of secrecy and the sacred itches of shame. The leavening qualities which art photography gives to the more exclusive pin-up mags was avoided for a long time.

Although Arthur Ferrier and numerous other draughtsmen had been working on the prototype for some time, it was the American artists Vargas and Petty who pumped up those lemon-mousse breasts to erectile bursting-point, polished those buttocks, inoculated pints of yellow colouring, tucked gauzes into corners, drawing them tight over nipples like rivets, described those imperative directive vees of creased underwear over hairless pubic mounds and arranged the whole amidst telephones and quilted satin across the fold-out pages first of *Esquire*, now of *Playboy*. But *Esquire* and *Playboy* were to relinquish the Vargas girl to other designers for she could never really be approached in her native penthouse. The governor's dream-secretary of the forties was stolen, trapped and transformed through the pages of magazines with a radically different quality. *Esquire* spawned

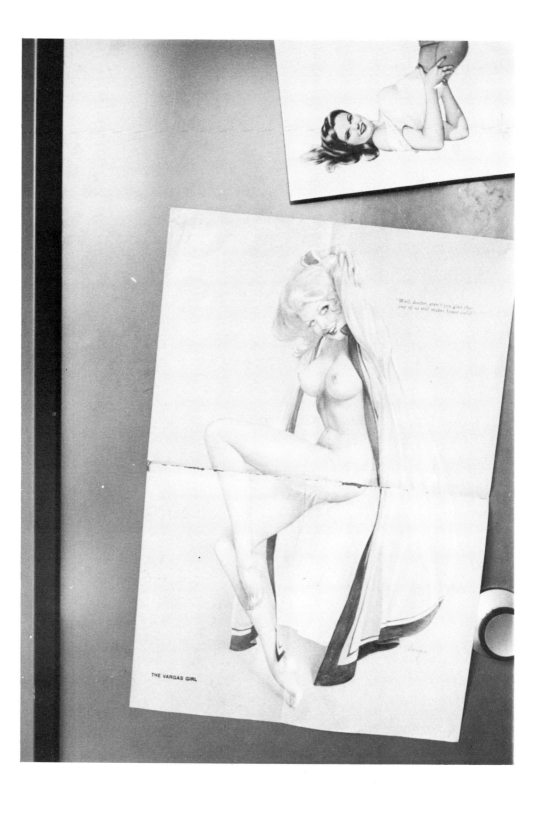

Well, doctor, aren't you glad that
one of us still makes house calls?

THE VARGAS GIRL

its boss-class family of copyists — *Playboy, Mayfair, Penthouse, Rogue, Nugget* —
who served up, along with art-writing of serious creative merit (presented as a
status symbol like the Mondrian on the office wall), a history of sun-kissed, free-
breathing bobby-soxers who had escaped from the Friday night hotel room where
Vargas's girl had frolicked, to the house party, the mixed swimming pool, the
organised wife-swap on thick carpets to the sound of the MJQ, and finally to
full-frontals in which the Mediterranean water sparkles on the bush and the sun-
tan extends uninterrupted right across budding mounds that could never in any
circumstances be called tits. There they began the dream-orgy which must be
banished back to dream if the real orgy, that of compression and transgressed
guilt, the fuck in which ecstasy is perpetually sweetened by revenge, is to survive.

*Men Only*, which had initially a kind of 8th Army officers' mess quality,
endows the girls with an air of the strip-club and the brothel. *Fiesta* is one amongst
a chain of magazines that alternate the girly pictures with short stories of the
torn-dress, run-out-of-petrol, only-one-bed-I'm-afraid variety, a tradition traceable
to the thirties magazine, *Razzle*, and beyond that to the very origins of farce. The
girl's ultimate destination was, however, the pages of countless pocket-size
magazines, the best of which is called *Spick and Span*. Here she drew closer
to the domestic slaughterhouse.

The unique quality of the *Spick and Span* picture is, in fact, the brilliant way
in which the atmosphere of immediate possibility is maintained. The girls are
surely carefully chosen so that they look like the wife, or like the wife used to

look. The thighs oozing over stocking-tops, the elaborate inelegance of the clothing, the glimpses of council-estate front rooms and motorway lay-bys behind the girls, the air of archness and callow self-consciousness which many of the models have, as though they feared for the cleanliness of their underwear, all add to the impression that these girls don't normally pose for photographers or lie around in their knickers. Consequently the stocking-tops, suspenders, G-strings, high heels and so on, far from belonging to the highly developed camp of the conscious fetishist, actually have the appearance of something *not meant to be seen*. They recall that swift and secret erection that occurred when the girl in the full skirt ran down the bus stairs too fast, when the self-conscious girl who blushingly agreed to get out of the car and walk over to the wood, caught her summer dress on the barbed wire. They recall the way the wife looked on the Costa Brava, or later when her new négligé arrived from Riviera Swimwear. Finally they recall those rows of shrieking matrons who rush in kaleidoscopes of Marks and Spencers lace and crammed nylon, across the gust of air in the seaside funhouse.

The girls in *Spick and Span* are in fact a triumph. The Vargas kitten, rich,

American, sophisticated, the strict property of the boss, has been kidnapped and tricked into the flesh of our own working women. The permutations of whores and pornographers would be tested hard to rival the undercurrents and overtones of excitement and power in that situation.

The dream-orgy, the Eden of the wealthy and the licentious, is spreading rapidly. Meanwhile the changing vocabulary of working-class eroticism may steal from it, and the theft will reliably follow the lines of the Vargas girl's fate.

She, but recently transformed into the stripper, the go-go dancer and the female impersonator, is herself in that role an agent whereby nakedness and homosexuality can be wrenched from the middle class. The progress from the drag act of twenty years ago, with its Hermione Baddeley-style camp and the inevitable Coward and Cole Porter songs, to Danny La Rue with his broad music-hall tartiness and the asides of a sceptical barman, is a swift and sudden route, from Mayfair and Soho to the East End pubs and thence to the Northern clubs and dying music halls where Peaches Page, 'Britain's Only Nude On A Bicycle', starred in shows like *Strip Strip Hooray* and *We've Nothing on Tonight*, because the strippers, few of whom have the cultural wit or power of the best drag performers, travelled alongside. Dicky and Dotty are marked exceptions. A husband-and-wife strip act, they have developed the business into an hilarious mime with hats, cups of tea and other objects replacing fig leaves and G-strings. In fact they use the strip situation in the different, fundamentally asexual, tradition of clown-conjur-

ing. Thus the eroticism of the nudity is disarmed and transformed by humour.

Similarly homosexuality is shielded by caricature. The difference between the flaming creatures of a West End drag club and the customers in the Hope and Anchor, Leeds, is one of humour. The homosexual labourers with their tattoos and mod suits and crude make-up are self-deprecatory dolls, as are the lesbians in their white collars and striped ties and black leather jackets. There isn't much doubt that working-class homosexuals see their homosexuality as a mark of some prestige, and have done so since long before the Gay Lib movement established itself, exploiting it as an area of heightened sensitivity whereby they surmount the butch qualities of the working domestic life. Thus the intonations of the male camp are amazingly close to the intonations of middle-class women taking tea in the Harrogate Pump Rooms. A formidable class loyalty, however, has to be represented, so the eyes roll and the little fingers lift with an exaggeration that brings a raucous and self-mutilatory humour to the proceedings. In any case, to have that margin in your identity which clowning provides is to sidestep the occasional blind violence of the slum protestant whose own homosexuality has been touched and therefore outraged.

Whilst the kidnapping is taking place and working people are learning that they can be homosexual without guying the part, that they can walk around the council house naked in mixed parties, even sleep together naked, the erotics of homosexuality and nudity are being coarsened, sharpened and strengthened. They must be endowed with the aesthetic grit necessary to penetrate the formidable numbness of fatigue that has to be surmounted amongst people for whom the central concern of life cannot be orgasm but must be food and work; for when the sexes are separated or taboos are otherwise lifted, eroticism itself dissolves and is replaced by a kind of aggressive fatalism in which the instinct, the genitals, the opposite sex itself, are all seen as the perpetrators of a vast practical joke simultaneously tricking a man or a woman into parenthood, which necessitates work, and teasing him with a desire unactable through fatigue. The dirty story is the expression of this. The peppering of language with the explosives 'fuck' and 'cunt' whenever the opposite sex is absent is a perpetual verbal invigoration which defies and defeats the humiliation possible in the battle between work and orgasm. The determination to continue fucking, to claim one's ecstasy beyond the nihilistic effects of the practical joke, is the naked face of a formidable erotic force that has nothing whatsoever to do with the power fetishes of the upper-class sado-masochist, a muscular and potent sexuality which the upper class, for all its knowledge and guiltlessness, is just beginning to covet. This is a significant reversal of envy. Not the kitsch of the gigolo guardsman or the cockney fashion model, but an important shift of aesthetic and therefore a promised shift of power.

# CLOTHES

The furore which occurred when councillors of one of the London boroughs discovered that they were using the rates to pay 'models' who posed in the nude for the students of the local art school, was based on the assumption that women are most sexually attractive when divested of clothing. Enclosed within this theory is another, that the 'models' were all beautiful and young. The reasoning goes something like: the purpose of art training is to learn to paint beautiful pictures, right? So if you get a beautiful woman and make a fair copy of her beauty in paint, the aesthetic will be transferred and you will automatically have a beautiful work of art. The notion that you could make a good work from a fat lady of sixty with pendulous breasts and chilblains simply didn't occur to them.

That clothing heightens rather than diminishes a woman's sexuality explains the vast quantity of erotic underwear that is now advertised, even in the most respectable of magazines. They emphasise the secret fear that, devoid of her feminine garments, a woman becomes too natural to be erotic. The prospective lover is cast in the role of voyeur, the image of the breast as an erotic object, the nipple pushing, thrusting, stretching, emphatically tense behind transparent wrappings, the panties with split crotch so that they need not be removed during coitus, placing the emphasis on the visual rather than the tactile sense. The hands of her lover will slip caressingly over nylon or silk, not her bare skin.

The National Socialist Party — the Nazi Party — had a fairly brief life in Germany in the thirties and forties, but in that period they achieved spectacular and cataclysmic results. It was — in current advertising jargon — extremely well presented. It seemed to spring into being fully-dressed, its image clear and expressive, typified by the archetypal Gestapo officer. He always appears the Dandy. His black uniform superbly cut, waist-hugging with neat leather holster, riding breeches and tight riding boots against which he would menacingly tap with a crop held in one hand together with a pair of black leather gloves. He was a figure to strike fear into anyone unfortunate enough to fall into his clutches, an intellectual with a will of iron, who despised weakness in lesser men. His boots always shine and glint in your eyes as the toe smashes into your teeth. On his blonde head he wears the dashing cap with the silver skull and cross-bones badge; high peaked at the front with the sides pulled down, the material soft and pliant. Thus the German people were confronted with this completed image of undisguised, unconcealed power. Nothing was hidden. The words of Hitler, the uniforms, the badges, banners, flags, said bluntly and uncompromisingly what they stood for. They cheered it, saluted it, supported it because it was so blatant it could not be true. The German designer seemed always to produce the exact image, the appropriate garment, which symbolised totally the brutal reality of the Party's policies. History applied as a gross varnish, Goering's sky-blue uniforms like the pale underbelly of a fighter aircraft, the swags of crosses round heroes' necks. The trappings of power and the pyjama-suited inmates of Belsen and Dachau with their gaudy ice-cream parlour stripes, ill-fitting and depersonalising.

Essentially we wear clothing to protect us from the climate. As a surrogate skin. Its secondary function, to conceal those parts of the body which are regarded as private or unmentionable, varies from time to time and place to place. The cod-piece of the Elizabethan, ostensibly a concealing device, drew the eye to the bulging, flaunting emphatic maleness of the wearer, his packaged genitals proceeding before him, a challenge to every woman. On the other hand, clothing which has a strictly utilitarian function, because it does not carry the token elements of the human body, is resistant to the process whereby clothing moves from being Fashion to becoming, with the passage of time, Costume. After the Second World War there was a turning away from the dull uniformity of wartime, an abhorrence of the trappings of Service, the uniforms and the monotony of khaki and navy blue. One notable exception was the duffle coat. Designed as protection for sailors on the convoys to Murmansk, no attempt had been made to express Admiralty views on uniform smartness or the Nelsonian traditions of the Royal Navy, by means of cut or styling. It was a democratising element, recognising the effect of the North Atlantic weather on the Lower Deck as well as the Ward Room. In Italy it became in the late forties the 'Montgomery' and the uniform of smart young men. In Britain the duffle coat became synonymous with University life, a unifying factor between Oxbridge and Red Brick — the first genuine student uniform for 250 years. It was as much a sign of intellectual inquiry as of studentship; worn equally by dons and undergraduates. And equally important, a sign of women's emancipation, the first post-war garment that was Unisex. It had been customary to separate patterns, weaves and colours according to sex. For some inexplicable reason men's coats were buttoned up with the left side over the right and women's the opposite way. Buttons had long been the focus of sexual attention, of the prelude to intercourse, the divesting of clothes, of women's blouses and men's flies. The duffle coat had none. Instead the primitive loop of coarse rope, the wooden toggle. No matter that the duffle coat was an extremely inefficient protection against wind: it conveyed a feeling of the outdoors, boats and rope, mountains and rocks; of comradeship and interdependence; trust and concern. And lastly it substituted the enveloping hood for the hat, so long a major signifier of social rank. It eliminated the separateness of the hat and diminished its importance.

There remain exceptions. The rep still must employ a hat when selling to the grocer, but he clutches it firmly in his hand, like a passport to respectability. The racing man must always go behatted, so that he may readily have the means to salute his superiors by its ritualistic removal, and they in their turn can acknowledge their inferiors by a twitch of the brim, or, to a lady, a gripping of the crown and removing from the head, the lady's status being defined with incredible accuracy by the amount of daylight between hat and head: for Her Majesty, complete removal and respectful bareheadedness; for all others, in measure of their social standing or degree of intimacy. It facilitates meetings and makes departures — the bane of British social life — simple and unembarrassing. Prince Philip never wears a hat when with his wife, British monarchs always.

On the famous occasion when the British monarch George IV visited Scotland, he adopted full Highland Dress. His intentions were, no doubt, to demonstrate an affinity with Scottish Life and Culture. He took the precaution of wearing flesh-

coloured tights to cover his bare knees and thighs though, as it was not customary to wear undergarments with the kilt. These also afforded a measure of modest concealment to the Royal Privates. The universal adoption of tights by women in the last ten years has disposed of one of the most erotic symbols of sexuality, the Suspender Belt. It has also disposed of the gap of naked thigh between the stocking top and the frilled knicker. The *illusion* of nakedness that the body stocking, the leotard and the ubiquitous tights provide, is in direct contrast to the *actual* availability of the wearer's body. The nylon or silk stocking — fully fashioned — left inviting chinks in the armour. They emphasised the body as flesh by all but concealing it. Each of the items of underwear had become lingerie, intended to be seen to conceal rather than deny what they hid. The wide bottom of the 'french' knickers, the strap and wire fastener, the dark reinforced top of the stocking, were all ambiguous false defences which demanded the manipulative skills of the fingers to unfasten and unlock. In contrast, paradoxically, the body stocking covers the body equally, pressing out and flattening the curves, concealing the body beneath a joinless carapace, offering no finger-holds, no points of weakness to be exploited, no access to the body's interior. With short skirts it was inevitable that the undergarment should be glimpsed. In order to combat voyeurism the knickers were desexualised — making them of figured

material normally associated with non-sexually loaded parts of the body or other objects such as curtains or cushions, and re-naming them panties or pantees, depriving them of the emotive naughtiness of the word knicker. This process whereby underwear loses its privileged secrecy of the domestic setting is a reversal of the fashion of the early twentieth century when undergarments were flesh-coloured, as though the skin of the woman's body had gone through an adaptive transmutation. Yet why camouflage corsets and brassieres to look natural when no one but the wearer will ever see them? It would suggest that the reason was more to do with the desensitising of difficulties experienced in purchasing them than in wearing them; a vague depersonalisation associated with surgical goods rather than a deliberate re-moulding of the body's shape to heighten its attractiveness.

The mass-production of clothes, the rapid adaptation of Haute Couture, has blurred the divisions between the classes as never before. The increased purchasing power of teenagers has given them a voice which they never before possessed. Style is democratic. The wealthy must rely on the quality of the material to distinguish them from the masses; even then they will boast that they always buy their underwear at Marks and Sparks. Moss Bros can still provide the ossified raiments of the past that the wedding demands. Women now demand The Look. The dress designer considers the whole woman, providing the cosmetics and the hairstyle consciously to create a statement that the woman can adopt and become. As the century draws towards its close, the past blurs into a series of crises. This is the first period of history when the actual events assume the meaningfulness of a chronicle. The appearance of the last 100 years is preserved on film and tape. We can re-live each moment of the immediate past. Only the present seems not to exist, to be without shape and devoid of language. So we invent appearances for it, ripping the images from the past, ignoring the economic and social conditions which gave them birth and significance, which they in fact embody. As the whole world seems to be locked in battle for the very survival of the human race, we are confronted with the bitterness of failure where all seemed triumph. Just when Man seems on the verge of believing that he can solve every question which he can pose, can overcome all his eternal enemies of disease and want, he comes face to face with himself, and in himself he finds his greatest, and perhaps his insuperable, enemy. Himself. So modern Industrial societies create new images of People, a mirror constantly searched for the real identity of a community become too complex to comprehend, reflecting our loss of confidence and our despairing fearfulness. The relationship between the individual and his values and the State to which he belongs, but no longer comprehends. What do the Modern Man and Woman really look like. Does that appearance hold the secret of the nature of our modern society, as we discern from the surface of past, encapsulated in film and photograph?

Each one of us has a clear notion of beauty. It is an ideal quality we associate with women. And those women who possess it, hold it in trust for all womankind. Being centred on the face, great beauty tends to reduce the possessor to the role of trustee. Great beauty takes on a quality of unattainable remoteness. The truly beautiful are rare. At a distance from us. Their mystery lies in our inability to comprehend their attractiveness. Men do not desire them carnally — great beauty is of the spirit, with the agelessness and innocence of perpetual youth.

The Beauty Contest is not a test of skill. However, the contestants are requested, from time to time during the event, to walk about. This they do awkwardly, their buttocks compressed, their thighs brushing at each self-conscious stride. The audience is exhorted by comperes to ogle them. 'Just move in so they can feast their eyes on your lovely beauty.' The girls (they are constantly referred to as adolescents, never as women) are clad in bathing suits. Each part of their body seems to contradict each other part. We, the audience, are made to feel our role as judges, adjudicating, discerning, deciding. But what are we trying to decide? As each girl is introduced we are aware that we are a higher court of appeal. Each wears round her body a banner proclaiming past success. Each has triumphed in battle against other girls, in town or country; others have paraded and been inspected and found deficient. The proud names roll out . . . Miss Manchester, Miss Wales, Miss Southampton, Miss England, Miss Bristol. What visions of municipal elections are conjured for us.

Soon these identifying labels are left off and once again the girls stride before us.

The air is filled with the curious strict tempo sound of a ballroom orchestra. The music is familiar and yet difficult to recall. What is that song? The Number One Hit of 1963. Tunes of a past decade follow, syrupy saxes smooth the way under the spotlights. The atmosphere is a blend of the ballroom and the circus, as in that moment in the big top — the Grand Parade — the ring master musters every bit of livestock the show possesses, and among the performing animals appear the menagerie beasts, who do nothing but contribute their presence.

So each girl assumes an air of intense ordinariness. We have been brought here to witness their femininity. High-heel shoes emphasise the naked leg, bunching the calves and straining the muscles of the thighs under the sun-kissed skin. The feet, the toes, are never seen unclad. The naked foot is too chaste in its natural state but encased in a high-heeled shoe it does not contradict the eroticism of the bared thighs. The whole torso is enveloped, encased, in a one-piece garment. It establishes immediately a legitimate reason for their state of partial undress. It is a kind of bathing dress seldom seen now on beaches or by swimming pools. The buttocks, their cheeks welded into one fused immobile mass, become a rump, a butt. The attention is focused on the silhouette, flattening the body, denying the sexual organs, barring the way to these hidden recesses, and one's attention is drawn thus more strongly to these erogenous zones made more desirable by the denial of their existence. The breasts are firmly encased in wire and cloth, shaped to a stereotyped hillock, denying their fleshliness, avoiding the faintest rhythmical undulation. These costumes are banal and familiar, with a faint air of chic. Purchased from the counters of Marks and Sparks, they are more suited to the bodies of older women. On these young girls whose bodies, we are assured, are lovely if we could but see them, they reassure the less well-endowed by eschewing their youthful advantage. They share a conspiracy of guilt by treating their bodies as objects in disguise.

The compere is a disc jockey. He questions each girl in turn. He tells us that the judges are looking for Personality as well as, yes, Loveliness. Now the TV camera pulls in and we concentrate on the personality field, the face. A wholesome sweetness pervades each girl. They all have quite presentable, even friendly, features, eager to

please, no pretensions to intellectualism. Their humble, ordinary lives are obscured by the titles by which they are addressed. They embrace the tinsel world of make-believe, they aspire to a vague showbiz future. None claims any special talent. In their earnest, nervous titters one discerns the anxious parent, the protective home, the carefully nurtured complacency.

The values of the world they are wooing are eagerly embraced. They cultivate a flat non-regional voice — unpretentious middle-class voice — not posh but careful, each word spoken properly. The questioner expresses astonishment when any of the finalists claims to have improbable interests or hobbies. Q: 'You're keen on chess?' His voice rises in crescendos of disbelief. He takes the audience into his confidence with a quick roll of his eyes. 'Who would you like to win, Fischer or Spassky?' He hesitates for a long Macarthyesque second. 'Fischer,' she assures him, shocked that he would throw doubt on her loyalty to the Free World. He defuses the question as a reward: 'Why? Because he's younger?' Back to the proper interests of such a lovely young creature — marriage prospects. To Miss Southampton, 'Just move in so they can feast on your lovely beauty.' He adopts the patronising air of the amateur pimp. No one strikes him down.

The audience, reminded of their voyeuristic role, concentrate on the girl's face, seeking to find in her nervous smile a mote of eroticism. All the girls are wearing identical make-up, false eyelashes, dark bright lipstick, but their eyes fail to signal deeper meanings than a desperate desire to be liked and their mouths smile, smile, smile, in virginal, unawakened hope. In all-unknowing contrast their hair tumbles about their shoulders, free and informal, pulling them once again into the household setting, bed-tossed and fingered, but as they turn under the glare of the spotlights the lacquer holds their coif in rigid discipline.

As each of the girls appears and disappears on cue, they seem to merge into one creature. The young man in the stage-cut evening dress puts another question. But first he pleads with the audience for their sympathy. 'This, as you can imagine, is no fun for me at all, talking to all these lovely young girls.' This lecherous aside is greeted with puzzled embarrassment. There are numerous prettier girls in the audience who are not in any apparent danger of attack. The suggestion that any girl with an atom of attractiveness is signalling willingness to roll on her back like a bitch in heat with any man is a new idea to them.

Mr Wogan returns to the attack. Miss Norwich has revealed a penchant for salmon fishing. 'That is a most unusual habit for a girl,' he states authoritatively. 'So what do you do, sit on the bank with the boyfriend and say nothing for hours and hours?' He leers lasciviously. 'Yes, for hours and hours.' Mr Wogan dismisses her story with ill-concealed scorn. He knows what Miss Norwich does when freed from the restraint of an audience and alone with a man. 'A likely story.' One is uncomfortably reminded that women who suffered assault and rape in the United States were ostracised socially and considered guilty by virtue of being found attractive enough to rape. Mr Wogan presses home the point. To Miss Manchester, 'Do you ever swim in that swimsuit?' 'There is always a first time.' 'If you win,' he promises, 'we'll go down to the pool and throw you in.'

The show stutters on towards its climax. One of these girls is to succeed to the title of Miss United Kingdom. The loveliest girl in the nation. The audience is totally confused. The contestants are so stereotyped that they merge into one cardboard cut-out image, without depth. It doesn't really matter now who is selected, it has become a lottery. The girls themselves are aware of this, of having abandoned themselves to luck. The result comes with a rush. A third and a second are announced and then to regal fanfare the choice is made. The throne is ready, the crown is produced and placed on the queen's head, and round her body, like a bat-cave label, the emblazoned title Miss United Kingdom. Sport is abandoned. No podium for the winner, this is selection by divinely guided acclamation. She has found a Career. She has won the right to share in the golden prizes of the fashion world. In one blinding stroke of fate she has been re-situated socially. Already she has been removed a little away from us. Now the other barriers are erected, large sums of money, a prize of £2,000, a guarantee of thousands of pounds' worth of work. Yes work, a vocation, travel, airplanes, as the list unfolds she recedes from the real world further. Soon the real world for her will be in reproduction, in photograph, to join the hierarchy of images, immobile, frozen and invulnerable. Making it.

# HAIR

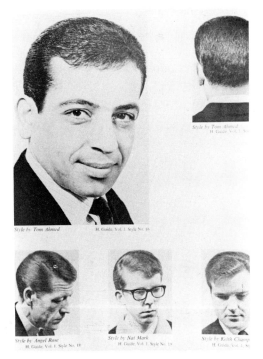

Style by Tom Ahmed    H. Guide, Vol. 1, Style No. 16

Style by Tom Ahmed
H. Guide, Vol. 1, Sty...

Style by Angel Rose
H. Guide, Vol. 1, Style No. 18

Style by Nat Mark
H. Guide, Vol. 1, Style No. 19

Style by Keith Champ
H. Guide, Vol. 1, Sty...

It is·part of the mythology of class differences that the working class is *physically* different from the 'upper' classes. Lord Peter Wimsey, as the archetypal aristocrat with socialist tendencies, exhibited all the infuriating *naturalness* of unselfconscious superiority. He contrived to appear classless because he was indifferent to the opinion of others. Whatever he wore, however he dressed — and it was invariably immaculate, *de rigueur* rather than *comme il faut* — he contrived a rightness, natural to a born leader. All aristocrats are depicted in fiction with long, loose, well-brushed hair, fitting the skull neatly without any apparent artifice — a fellow must never appear to have just had his hair cut — rather long at the front so that it may fall over one eye to assist cogitation; a noble alternative to thinking. The working-class stereotype is possessed of a substance more resembling scrub. It rises from the scalp in even length, *en brosse,* resisting all attempts to quell its unruly aboriginal nature. It must be fashioned, styled, loaded with meaning, and it must demonstrate its contrived form- ality. The hair is worn like a distinguishing cap with numerous cross-references to categorised activities, sport, cinema, the business world. The well-groomed head carries the image of ambition, an accommodating conformity which will pay off, an adaptive camouflage of assumed gentility masquerading as urbanity. These hair- styles act as grafts, a magical association with the touchstones of sexual success, aggressively male, designating women as objects responding intuitively to the correct visual code. The aura of the surgery which pervades the barber's shop, the white coats, the sharp shiny instruments, the pinioning of the arms under the all-enveloping sheet, the surrender to the manipulating, intimate touching fingers. The image returned from the mirror. The disembodied head, the face anxiously surveying the transformation process to irresistibility — sell it, sell it. The furtive exchange of money after the stiff-legged rise from the chair, the brothel-smells of conspiratorial scents, the display of Durex, sensitol rubbers, the hopeful purchase to allay the fears of the aroused female, helpless before the blatancy of his tonsorial sexual signals, the dream-world of surfaces, the copying book of social ascent.

The hair is a convenient signalling system. At the Olympics of recent years the American black athletes have proclaimed their aroused political, ethnical awareness of their African origins by a flaunting frizzy black cloud of hair, Afro-style, the mythical naturalness of the real African, resistant to white socialising value judgments, proclaiming 'Black is Beautiful', eschewing their Americanism. The real Africans' hair is short, cut close to the scalp, conformist, tribal and neat, many of them soldiers and policemen, at one with their society, supporters of their leaders. They would regard such exotic hairstyles as primitive and peasant, a class sign rather than an ethnic one.

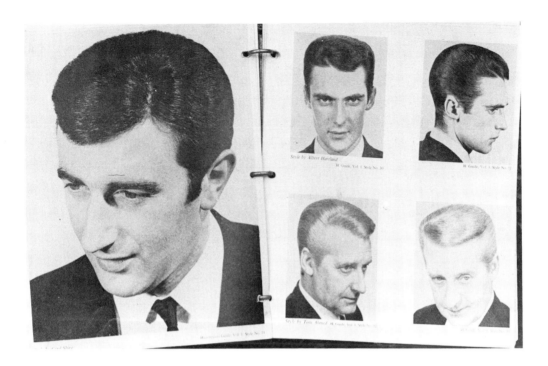

Many explanations have been offered for the presence of hair on the human body in the patches they cover — under the arms, the head and the genitals — none of them satisfactory. Underarm hair is thought unsightly in women. The naked armpits of Rita Hayworth were amongst the most erotic images of the fifties. Accumulating by subtraction. Conjuring the unthinkable and the unmentionable. By the deliberate erasure of an innocuous area, all body hair is charged with erotic meaning. The hair which so adorned Miss Hayworth's head — red, signifying her independence and boldness — hung in languorous freedom over her face, at once a veil and shield and a tumbled invitation to bed. In the fifties 'going to bed' was a euphemistic fuck; sleeping with someone was being very much awake, as though sex demanded the scenario of domesticity.

It is a strange paradox that while Samson's strength lay in his luxuriant locks, armies all over the world inculcate militant aggressiveness by the application of the clippers to the back of the recruit's neck. Today, the Patriarchs go bare-faced and the Youth bearded; the rejection of one kind of conforming anonymity produces another. The hippies, the yippies, the skinheads, the teds, the head-shavers and the hair-growers proclaim their spiritual allegiances *publicly*, for hair lends itself readily to evangelism. Hairstyles demand converts, simplify issues, demarcate, and reject consensus.

# CHEZ NOUS

Many a gentleman of the old school has been provoked to remark regretfully upon the underbred manners and bearing of even the better classes in the modern industrial communities; and the decay of the ceremonial code — or as it is otherwise called the vulgarisation of life — among the industrial classes proper has become one of the chief enormities of latter-day civilisation in the eyes of all persons of delicate sensibilities. The decay which the code has suffered at the hands of a busy people testifies — all depreciation apart — to the fact that decorum is a product and an exponent of leisure-class life and thrives in full measures only under a regime of status.

Thorstein Veblen

The qualities of subtlety are the signatures of dying. Thus when we experience them we weep. The exquisitely placed motif, the barely perceptible curve, the delicate warping of symmetry, the close harmony or the contrived discord of closely pitched tones and colours are noble, esoteric, and constitute the language of a highly refined sensibility. So axiomatic do these merits seem that it is important to examine their considerable negative aspect, their death aspect.

The duality which can only be seen by a refined sensibility is *difficult to see*. The esoteric quality is *not much use to most people*. Nobility is incorrupted. Being incorrupted, it is inexperienced. Nobility is *naïve*. Nobility has never dirtied its hands, perhaps because *it has never had to*.

Subtlety, then, in its necessary precision, is a scaling down of awareness. It is the language of people who see well the barely perceptible because the obvious pains them. The subtle detail presents itself sharply because a certain myopia has denied the panoramic, the epic or the extravagant.

Finally the subtle gesture is an economy of failing energies. Those gentle arabesques are the cultivated skill of workmen who can no longer address themselves to the full circle. When executed on a large scale, in the English country house, they are carried out by employees whose native language is significantly different.

It could be said, then, that subtlety is the special contrivance of a sensibility refined by failing energy. It is the high skill of the enfeebled élite.

The living populace, in their perpetual coveting of leisure and status, seize form as they seized the Vargas girl, and transmute it so that it expresses the wider

compass of their energies. Marble they will have in granite. Granite they will have in concrete. Bronze they will have in plaster. Porcelain in plastic. The translation into cheaper materials carries with it that invigoration of cultural statement that indicates why the one material is the property of the élite and therefore expensive, and why the other is the property of the mass and therefore cheap. Not merely a matter of rarity and plenitude but also a question of the myopic sensibility refusing coarse grain which it finds actually painful. This being perceived, clear stages of cultural escalation begin to be seen.

Colours are powerful. The suburban garden is a statement of bold primary colours and the same reds, yellows and blues trumpet forth throughout the first two stages of escalation. They are the colours of work. The straight, bright paint of lorries, vans, buses, postal services, uniforms, regimental insignia, hand tools, agricultural machinery, building machinery and all the wrappings and advertisements that belong close to work. The windows of gardening shops, hardware shops, radio shops, electrical equipment shops, the sales catalogues of agriculture and industry, are heraldic in the *simplicity* of their colours.

In the second level they are the colours of play. Dolls, toy vehicles, swings, seesaws, slides, roundabouts and the procession of goggling anthropomorphic animals are coloured in bright, simple dyes. The bestiary, bleeding off on the right into the high subtleties of Beatrix Potter's watercolours and on the left into the douce gradations of colour in Walt Disney's movies, marks the possession of distinction on one hand and the envy of it on the other. Both groups of posturing pets were drawn back into the discordant centre of primary play by being cast in plastic and coloured with stencilled dye. Disney's premature attempt to join hands with Kenneth Grahame and A. A. Milne opened a sewer of cultural discord it would be hard to surpass. The primary colours are also, at the second stage, the colours of carnival, of Christmas decorations, fairy lights, party squeakers, silly hats, flashy ties, holiday dresses and trouser suits, bathing costumes and saucy knickers.

Throughout the first two stages, then, the simple aesthetic can be maintained.

Blunt and bright with forms and structures that have the brute functional punch of a pair of pliers with its handles sheathed in orange plastic, or the bulbous breast-and-buttock humour of a piggy-bank.

The straight, blunt statement is possible because through Stage One and Stage Two the taboos between the sexes and between the classes are undeveloped or temporarily dropped. When the sexes come together in the home, when the tensions of erotic compression are high and the aspiration towards status is a sore point of emotional leverage between the sore bodies of disappointed partners, then the colours and lines of subtlety have to be attempted and the aesthetic accumulates its full gaudy potency.

I am walking down a steep cobbled street in Bradford. The terrace back-to-backs are busy with dirty children, women dashing in and out in turbans and mules from which the lilac shades are somewhat faded, hanging their washing on the lines that bar the street to traffic. The sun beats down on suds and gutter filth and the confetti of sweet wrappings, cigarette cartons, beer cans, paper bags, lost shoes, dropped comics, clinging around drains originally sunk in the middle of the road to take all the domestic refuse of a hundred years ago, when the entire working class dwelt at the utilitarian First Stage, the level for which these caves were designed. The litter of the street is a layer of the Second Stage thinly covering the First, an archaeological stratification, still above ground.

The doors are open and glimpses into the houses reveal no peasant flagstones and scrubbed boards, not even the cracked linoleum and newspaper tablecloths of some short time since. Within, the Third Stage has been achieved and flowers in full glory. Each domestic glimpse is a cameo of seascapes and sunsets and jungles and forests and gossamer gowns and shimmering lagoons, all expressed in plastic flowers, lampshades, wallpapers, framed prints, calendars, carpets, cushions, furnishings, windowglass, mirrors, all of it new, shining, the pale subtleties of the aristocratic lawns won back into a vigorous romanticism where a young wife could perhaps recline in a plastic leopardskin catsuit, and the mawkish moanings and purrings of love extravagant enough to be sentimental can find their lyrical colouring properly displayed. And halfway down the street, where the stairs rise steeply only three feet within a door that bears a Japanese sunrise in strips of ply, there is a new stairs carpet. It is the colour of the flame within the rose. The range of brooding lovers' blood. But it has stronger messages than this. The tongues of flame brighten right round the spectrum to a yellow as bright as egg-yolk, and the smouldering shadows deepen to the blackest shade of hell. And, that the stridency of these colours might not be lost, the whole length and breadth of this is held down step by step with the stairs rods *on top of* the cellophane in which the carpet was delivered.

It is a pointed statement of the front-room mentality in a one-room house, for although the shitty nappies pile up in the back room of a two-room house and the dartboard hangs amongst its peppering of holes, and the bicycle stands against the back of the caved-in settee, although Dad sits with his collar off and his Woodbine smoking, with his stockinged feet on the mantelpiece between the tin alarm clock and the brass stallions that Granny left us, the *front* room must not be entered except on Sundays and Bank Holidays, and then only if we put on our best clothes. Once there we lose the dry rasps of fatigue and the short expletives of common speech, rather as we do when on holiday. But it is a different kind of style we cultivate in the front room from the one we cultivate at Butlin's. This is the place where we entertain the older generation of the family, who are pensioned at Stage One under the wing of the chapel, or happily landed at Stage Five with a royal portrait over their mantels. This is where we glance forward to the Fourth Stage, of ostentatious success, or the Fifth Stage of ostentatious Protestant respectability. This is where we prove that, far from letting the family down we are advancing in taste and respectability and status. We are, in fact, advancing faster than they did. What will they have to drink? Whisky? Gin? Egg flip? Or just a beer? It's only Christmas once you know. And how's the shop doing, George?

Throughout the first half of the twentieth century, front rooms were the

standing galleries for a succession of artefacts that were intended to mark the
sophistication of the householder but which despite his intention continued to
express his continuing vigour. As the Italian boy, either whistling or with cherries,
gave way to the Art Deco lady athlete in jade who in turn gave way to the
windswept Diana of the Uplands with her twin retrievers, her picture hat
and her summer dress; as the retrievers grew into plaster Alsatians, some of
whose eyes ignited like ghost hounds, and Diana became the ecstatic nude, more
comely yet than her shallow-breasted saltwear ancestor of the twenties, as those
lyrical lines were abstracted into a piece of glass modern art in which the bubbles
were frozen in a tide of Raspberry Tizer; as the plates bearing the three-colour
images of vintage cars replaced the plates that had born the ponderous reliefs of
cottage gardens and Devon villages, then lustre-wear fish wafted out of the
redundant glass cabinet, escaping their prison of ground-glass panels, to play
delirious games with light on a minute plastic wall-shelf over the tank where
actual tropical fish lived out their exotic lives beside the new three-speed hi-fi.
And by this time the front room was no longer a front room but one room with the
wall knocked down between front and back, with a serving hatch into the kitchen;

and those Sunday rituals at which we had all sat at the edges of our seats had, here and there, given way to different rituals whereby we lounged against the cocktail bar of plastic bamboo with our Bacardi in glasses around whose walls huntsmen chased one another, or maybe vintage cars, or maybe more tropical fish. But the purpose of the ritual was the same and instead of maintaining cramped silences as we refused another tongue sandwich at Stage Three, we now dropped casual remarks about our holiday in Majorca while we refused another chicken vol-au-vent at Stage Four. Meanwhile the lustre fish on his plastic shelf protects our vitality even as we threaten it, in our emblazoned blazers and our club ties. Along his scales the turquoises and violets, the crimsons and the golds, the very defining hues of exoticism and romance, are so blended as to clash with a pointed virulence more poignant and more powerful even than the primary colours we left at work; those graceful curves will sacrifice the attempted subtlety by coming too close to the letter 's', and the light of those glistening over-profuse highlights will reflect on to the muted, artificially muddied barrel of the vacuum-mould blunderbuss over the built-in electric fire, on to the subtle varnish of the fawn, hand-carved in natural wood, leaping across yet another plastic shelf.

It is not a matter of wealth. Impecunious students can construct interiors of real subtlety and taste from junk shops and evening classes whilst Lady Docker and the Burtons spend thousands. It is a matter of our having chosen the blend, the broadening, the simplifying of subtlety that finally pleases our ebullient senses the more. We have no wish to greet neighbours or relatives with a graceful dip of the head and an ironic remark. We continue to extend a handclasp and a big hello. Our fathers fed us through unemployment, strikes, wars, and we are going up in the world *together*, even if I am doing a bit better than you of course, and our Edith's going out with a fella from London with two cars.

It is this sense of escalating together that disappears in puddles of competitive respectability in dormitory villages at the Fifth Stage. From those rose-spangled villas the secure lower middle class looks down and refuses admittance. From those ritzy plastic interiors the working class looks up, their sensibilities still lively with the breadth that comes from work and squalor sustained through generations of oppression, systematically vulgarising the cultural vocabulary of the middle class as they appropriate it, invigorating each wave of supercilious taste and patronising education that is hurled at them either to absorb them or thrust them back.

The taste for ornament that rushes in when the First Stage utilitarianism of the kitchen table and the iron bedstead has been surpassed, milked history throughout the twenties, thirties and forties. Pickford's vans drove down countless suburban streets to unload Jacobean chests on which cavaliers might have

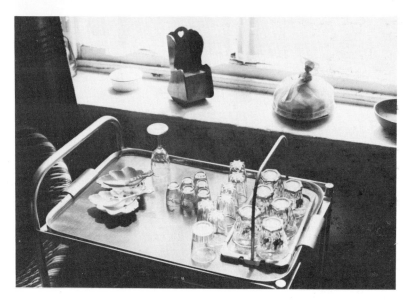

roistered, Japanese gate-leg tables with Romanesque mouldings, Welsh dressers with Egyptian columns and Greek vases on the doors, Romantic suns squared up by the Cubists, cast in plaster by cinema architects and emulated in the wood of modernistic armchairs, record players, cocktail cabinets, sideboards. The Festival of Britain, with its swift inoculation of Bauhaus functionalism, geometry, and Scandinavian natural qualities, was soon wrested from the hands of the taste crusaders by the coffee-bar proprietors who put sexy negresses on the earthenware cruet, replaced the Ostwald colours on the screen panels with pastel-shade gloss, painted the wooden walls black and decorated them with Caribbean landscapes, or skylines of New York, in luminous paint.

From then it was a short step to G-plan furniture, screw-on 'ebony' chair-legs, chromium and glass coffee tables, multiple wallpapers whose *tachiste* patterns could easily be transformed from tasteful close tones in green and purple to reliable colours like ochre and gilt.

Thus it would blend with the graining on the woodwork in the hall, and the coffee table only needed a galleon under its glass top to look even more exciting with the old three-piece suite and the new Bernard Buffet print of a sad clown.

Or perhaps if we took the Buffet back to the shop we could get a Tretchikov native girl, the one with the bilious green face, and then we could hang up the Chianti bottles we brought back from Capri. Anyway the horse galloping out of the waves wouldn't fit.

Scandinavian design was a formidable piece of subtlety, a bold and courageous move to involve the mass of people in devitalised gestures. It would perhaps not be too extravagant to suggest there was a mystery to the process whereby the common condition reasserted itself and the overall effect of the Contemporary interior was exactly that of one of Frank Randle's gastric accidents.

# DOORS

Gates and doors divide, subtract, terminate, retain and exclude. Mill gates keep out intruders, create a separate world of manufacture, of industry, an enclave of reward, where money is to be had. The gates protect the wage-earners from the outside world. They also contain them and control them. The front door of the suburban city-dweller is separated from the public highway by his front garden; not so the inhabitant of the residual Victorian terraces. Strangers brush past his door steps, he is within arm's reach. His front door is his one and only line of defence. It guards the hall and the

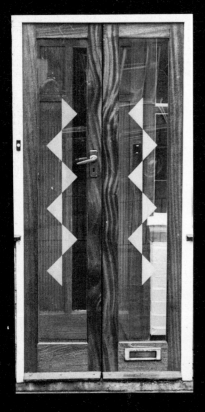

intimate areas of the house. It proclaims the identity of the household. Often it was the only concession to middle-class taste, the oval window a glow of cathedral-like splendour, a leaded-glass ripple of representational 'Art', flowers, leaves, shields and vaguely heraldic devices, all of absolute symmetry. Adaptations of a DYS distinction appear as the neighbourhood sinks down the social scale, a rejection of the fussy signs of 'antiquity', a covering over of panels and a token gesture of newness, an offset pattern, a deliberate asymmetry. As a district comes back into fashion new doors appear, woodenness reappears — one cut above the grained door — or the confident glass panel bearing a seascape complete with argosy, and a tacit avowal of house-pride.

# PUBS

The slab, cut like a slice of ham from a tree, constitutes the modern equivalent of the brass plate or the moulded wooden notice. Until recently every piece of wood used in the interior of a building was processed with classical mouldings, transforming the wood into style and denying naturalness. The slice of tree is detimberised, planed to an un-natural smoothness, the edges softened, the transition from plane to plane rhythmically eased. Here in the Crown Hotel is proclaimed simplicity, old-world comfort, atmosphere, the black Gothic script redolent with the basic goodness of the simple life of the monk, slightly biblical, heraldic and regal, all fused together by the directness of the *objet trouve* nature of the label. It prepares us for the stage-set bar, the lounge like the setting for act one of a Whitehall farce, everything contrived to look part of an organic and perpetual growth. It is Publicans' Tat out of the Daily Mail Ideal Homes crossed with Barry Bucknell and lampshades from British Home Stores.

# WMC

The architect is employed to give expression to aspirations. The aspirations of the WMC are realised in the building which constitutes the centre for their social activities. The original N.W. Ward Liberal Club 'premises' revealed its political origins in its union affiliations. Now their friend is Mr Webster the brewer. Goodfellowship is expressed in companionable drinking. The WMC is a family affair, a social club.

Bright wallpaper with large, bold, modern designs covers the walls — no two adjoining walls bear the same design, emphasising the joins where wall meets wall in precise right angles. There are thick curtains flanking the panoramic windows — no small panes here — and the discreet repetition of the brewer's name. The prosperity of the club rests on the bar profits. It is an ideal partnership between labour and commerce. The drinking, which is heavy and sustained, is blessed by the obvious benefits accruing from the bar profits. No drunkenness is permitted and indeed is frowned upon by all members. The drink revives old memories rather than erasing awareness. They are proud of their new club. It has lost its frowning frontal aspect, it now stands in its own grounds. Brick has lost its proletarian significance, it is warm and familiar, 'real' and unpretentious. While the style is not brutal it attempts an appearance of 'newness' by its 'non-style', but it essentially reassures by its air of domesticity.

# CAKE

There is a universal assumption that a developed taste in food and drink means an appreciation of a wider range of sensations other than sweetness. The use of sweeteners is now so widespread in prepared food that there is an association, which is rarely questioned, between the degree of sweetness and the level of enjoyment. Sweetness is a reward. Children are bribed by it, adults ultimately comforted by it.

This universality of Taste, this association of the taste of sugar with infancy, with conformity, obedience and love, has become, by association, a quality of femininity. A woman who rejected this truth, this fondness for sweetness, would have to provide sound reasons for her exceptional attitude. It must appear as a sacrifice: for dietary reasons, Doctor's Orders, or any other conforming excuse. It must be in a spirit of self-sacrifice, the cost of beauty, the price of constant vigilance that woman must pay to maintain her attractiveness. The sticky sweet drinks that assume a celebratory pretence and allow gentility by a token toast, exclude women from the conviviality of drinking for drinking's sake. These are dessert wines, sweet sherry, syrupy concoctions, a natural adjunct to meals. They allow the drinker to imbibe without consequence, to join in without losing the privilege of detachment, to sip rather than gulp. It is the standpoint that states that Taste is natural and not acquired. These are the drinks of the working-class woman or girl. The girl is aware that the pub is man's territory — she is tolerated. Under the protection of her escort she sips Babycham, a child again, drinking a sham drink which denies its potency behind its pseudonym, with its nudging hints of respectability, of weddings and toasts to the bride and groom in real champagne perry. These drinks disassociate themselves from drunkenness. Intoxication is not the aim. If it occurs as a consequence, the condition is irrationally ascribed to some other cause. 'She can't be drunk, she hasn't had a drink all night, not a proper drink, like. Only seventeen Babychams and you can't get pissed on that stuff.' It was undoubtedly something she ate.

This proletarian lack of sophistication in the matter of food and drink can be seen as an enviable closeness to Nature — as the sign that the true nature of 'Nature' is sweet. This fundamentalism which readily confuses sophistication with intellectualism seeks to deliver the bored from the tedium of Taste by conferring on substances such as honey a magical power to convert the user back to a Nature created to sustain Man in perpetuity. The simplicity of taste of the working classes can then be seen as an enviable state of grace — the possession of a natural virility which is an ample recompense for the unremitting labour of their lives.

A love of sweets is generally ascribed to women collectively. It is part of her womanliness. She is possessed by it. It is part of her fundamental nature — she has a sweet tooth, and to deny it is to deny her naturalness. She prefers 'fresh' butter to salted butter, cream cakes to meat pies, raspberry jam to bloater paste, chocolate to peanuts, and trifle to cheese and biscuits. The coercive nature of sweetness involves women in a conspiracy of conformism. It excludes them from the world reserved by men. To break out of this rigid convention implies a whole change in a woman's role — the young girl who achieves a university place will shock and horrify her working-class parents by calling for a pint of bitter, by eating steak rather than the symbolic chop, by spurning the sweet for the cheese, and preferring Brie or Camembert at that.

In marked contrast to Continental countries Britain does not have cake shops. The Baker — the Baker's shop — the Bakery, produce the full range of the oven's products, for baking is the alchemy of the kitchen. The ingredients are the very stuff of the Land. Flour, butter, lard, dried fruits, yeast, salt and sugar are all distinguished by their natural elemental character. The magical change is brought about by fire, heat, warmth, and they are transmuted into nourishing food. Bread, bearing as it does the colour of its benevolent fusion with fire, is the symbol of a bountiful co-operation between the Gods and Man.

The cake, on the other hand, belongs in a fairy-land. A world of dreams, of heightened sensations where all is overstated. Cakes are almost pure Language. They appeal to the mind, the emotions, rather than the body. Their visual appearance is exaggerated to exorcise all subtleties. It is a flight from Nature. The structure can be rigid, mathematically exact, a construction of parts where the ornamentation overwhelms its 'support' — that is, the body of the cake — and ultimately dispenses with it altogether. It becomes total ornament. Becoming total ornament it becomes the 'cake' which in turn must be further ornamented. Small cakes are like children's toys in the shop rather than in the child's hands. They achieve their apotheoses when they

are purchased. But the tragedy of the toy is that, once into the hands of the child, it is abused by use; its complexity beyond the child's conception, he must destroy it. Since most toys are almost totally *visual* extensions of the appearance of the adult world rather than the function which dictated that appearance, they really work best as objects to be looked at rather than handled. So too cakes. The 'food' element is entirely concealed under layers of icing, splodges of cream, with gaudy nipples of cosmetised cherries, squiggles of chocolate in incomprehensible hieroglyphics. The calligraphy of eastern pottery squirms over pink, yellow and white shiny surfaces often brutally confronted with a piece of real fruit, a strawberry rendered unreal and inadequate in its pulpiness, its messiness, in contrast to the hard, perfect surfaces. These confections are the antithesis of nourishment. They are the embodiment of excess, of a revolt against the necessitous meal. The eating of them is pure anti-climax. They are pervaded with a cloying sweetness. Sticky and intractable they clog the teeth and fur the tongue. They are satisfying only in that their beautification,

having been admired, can on the instant be destroyed.

Of the larger cakes the layer type fulfils the desire to turn a meal into a celebration. The sponge cake, demonstrating a degree of honesty, reveals in its lop-sidedness the secret processes of the oven. Belching cream from the slit in its side, it bespeaks a generosity, a reckless profligacy somewhat spoiled by the artificiality of the filling. It is one of the paradoxes of their calling that baker shops call cream, 'real cream', to distinguish it from artificial cream, which is called simply 'cream'. This natural 'real cream' is different from the simulated type in that it has no image of creaminess, so its advertised 'realness' puts it into a different category. It becomes beneficial and nourishing by moving out of the single-dimensional world of appearance into the multi-dimensional world of Nature, evoking farming, dairies and, ultimately, cows.

The apogee of confectionery art is the wedding cake. The rigidity of the formal aspects of weddings is due in large measure to the desire of the lower classes, the aspiring working classes, for respectability. A concession to the mores of the lower stages may be made by the defiant wearing of 'lounge suits', and the use of the Registrar's Office rather than the Church, but the cake is never neglected. With the decline of the custom of the 'dot' or dowry, the middle class demonstrates its wealth by the lavishness of the wedding, customarily the expense falling on the father of the bride. As the dividing line between the lower and middle class has become blurred, so these customs of the middle class have ritualised into the 'norm' — the right thing. Woe betide the family, no matter how slender its means, who cannot provide its daughter with a resplendent ceremony. The whole standardised event, commercialised down to the last place setting. The cake holds pride of place. Rising tier over tier, like a fanciful example of stockbroker-classical architecture, solid and well-founded, it is surmounted by the tiny simulacra of the bridal pair, posed in frontal exposure like a 3-D photo. The un-natural, inorganic, man-made structure of the cake is strewn with trinkets and tokens of de-mythologised magic, their natural appearance partly destroyed by rendering them all in silvery metallic paint. Shoes, horse-shoes, heather, blue-bells and forget-me-nots, storks, babies and bows, prepare the couple for any eventuality, reminding them in a genteel way of their responsibilities as future parents. A solemn and chilling note sounded amidst the fairy-tale romanticism of the occasion. The cake is stabbed four-handed, the structure demolished and disarmed, its dismantled layers divided among the guests in wrappings of tissue, or dispatched to distant and absent friends that they may assess the substance of the cost embodied in the weighty lump of crumbling cake with its subcutaneous layer of fatty marzipan and its armoured hide of hard, brittle icing. One of the tiers of cake is traditionally kept for the first anniversary, emphasising the cake's magical powers to defy time and still remain wholesome enough to serve as christening cake for the first-born.

# HARRY RAMSDEN

Harry Ramsden sold fish and chips. The finest in the country he claimed, and who would dispute it. The potato is a staple part of the diet of the British, and the 'chip' is its vulgar role. The rating of a restaurant can be assessed by the terms it employs to sell its potato dishes. 'Pommes frites' is exotic and places the vegetable in that category of food in which dwells 'Steak Diane', escargots and a nice glass of bodjers. French fries are coffee bar, Wimpyesque and often squiggly in shape, while 'chipped potato' is precise in description, undisputably the garden variety and rejoicing in a splendid name. None of these vegetable dishes is in the competition.

Ramsden's is the corner 'chipper', elevating the whole process of eating food from a paper bag to the status of dining out. From the original simple 'Harry Ramsden' above the door, the numerals on his clock (time for tea) replaced by the twelve letters of his name, the simple conceit of the shopkeeper, the establishment has become known as . . . what? Is it Harry Ramsden's . . . restaurant? Or cafe — bistro — fish bar — snack bar — eatery — diner? He doesn't claim any of these titles. He provides a

bridge of nostalgia for the working-class aspirant to middle-class values, a bridge back to the necessitous commonality of cheap hot food, the short commons of the inter-war period, the shame of working women deprived of their domestic role.

Chippers never opened during the day in Scotland but provided the euphemistically named 'Supper', the supplementary meal, an indulgence rather than a dietary necessity. Harry Ramsden's, even though cast into the hands of MacFisheries, brings a kind of glory to such pride.

SHOPPING LIST

| | |
|---|---|
| Fish | 400,000 pounds. |
| Dripping | 150,000 pounds. |
| Potatoes | 900,000 pounds. |
| Sauce | 20,000 bottles. |
| Tea | 6,000 pounds. |
| Butter | 13,000 pounds. |
| Bread | 26,400 loaves. |
| Milk | 84,000 pints. |
| Sugar | 14,000 pounds. |
| Salt | 2,000 pounds. |
| Vinegar | 9,000 pints. |

Harry Ramsden

Some of the ingredients needed to satisfy over a million customers a year, which makes Harry Ramsden's the most famous Fish & Chip Shop in the world.

# STEW

The butcher's shop in Scotland disassociates itself from the abattoir. Instead of readily identifiable parts of animals, the customer finds carefully rolled anonymous packages. Wrapped and strung like Christo art works, they assume a form more akin to tree sections, the alternating rings of pale pink and white forming soft annular rings. The dissection is done in the back of the shop, furtively, like an eighteenth-century anatomy lesson. The bones are cut away, the structure of the animal disrupted, the armature which sustained the flesh is dismembered. It ceases to be animal, it becomes flesh; indeed above the door is not 'Butcher' but the title 'Fleshing'. An enquiry as to the reason for this avoidance of the signs of carnage, the obscuring of the mortality of the animals, elicits the explanation that it was a contingency of the Second World War. Out of a spirit of fairness, when meat was in short supply and rationed by weight and the greatest demand was for the rear, choice parts of the beast, the corpse was dismembered and reduced to tatters. Thus none could tell one part from another, and the meat was fit only for stews and the like.

Stewed meat is very much a part of the working class in Scotland. In it meat loses all evidence of its origin. It is a communal food. It surrounds the eater with the warmth and comfort of home. It is long in the preparation and betokens careful planning, concern in the cooking, constant tasting and decision-making. It is nourishing and sustaining, and the cooking imparts the flavour and strength of the meat to the vegetables. Until recently steak rarely appeared on the table of the working-class home. For reasons of economy undoubtedly at times. But steak holds a deeper meaning. Its rawness threatens. When it is cooked, it is no longer under the control of the cook. It seems to come to life, as though it were dormant. The juices flow from it, red and rich. It induces a heady madness, an excess of explosive energy, a recklessness that threatens the family. It combines at once in its rawness and the simplicity of its preparation a foreignness, an exoticism that threatens the intrusion of 'foreign' ways. As it is eaten it isolates the eater, sets him apart from his companions. The flesh becomes his flesh in the instant, no intermediate digestive process seems necessary. The good Scots wife knows that the thick brown gravy that glazes over the complex melange of meat and veg, is the best of all worlds, the long marathon, the careful husbanding of strength and resources for rough waters which undoubtedly lie ahead.

# SLOP

The vulgar sensibility, then, is bared first by accident and secondly, it having been exposed, by celebration. Drill Sergeants, Masters of Ceremony, bus conductors, policemen giving evidence, all attempt an upper-class accent and arrive at a discordant cultural fusion that expresses even more graphically the mood of their original dialect.

'Well your worship, Hai was a-walkin' dahn Helbert Street habaht 'alf-an-hour hafter closin' teyme' — or 'If thet fahkin' menn thah hon the front renk dewn't git 'is fahkin' harms swingin' Hei'll 'eve 'is fahkin' guts for fahkin' gahtahs!'

The front room attempts subtlety and achieves a more pointed vulgarity. That vulgarity adopted consciously becomes the conspicuous *style* of Diana Dors or Lady Docker.

The components of the quality are common guts and vulgar exuberance accentuated by juxtaposition with their opposites, taste and subtlety and distinction. It is perceived by the way the opposite impulses sour one another, the bright purple getting into the violet mists to produce mauve or 'aubergine'. The bright red getting into the cerise to produce knicker-pink. The back-door green getting into the sage of distant meadows to produce an 'emerald hue'.

If the moral essence behind good taste is nobility, harmony, love and trans-cendant death, the discordant aesthetic that advertises life and betrays the people's advance towards subtlety is most sharply and pungently seen not so much in sex, or in decor, but when people who spend most of their time at the material business of hard work and penny-pinching lurch into the nobler emotions. When they fall in love. When they celebrate family loyalties. When they wed. When they pray. When their loved ones die.

Sentimentality is that contemplation of grace that refuses to acknowledge the price whereby grace is won, that refuses to acknowledge death.

The art of peasants in a static servility can celebrate death with no senti-mentality. Folklore is full of death myths and death images handled with high poetry. The rising populace, however, is so roaringly alive it must rhyme the lovers' moon with June, must roar 'Abide With Me' at football matches, plant Christmas trees on children's graves and mass-produce Christ in plastic.

It is Sunday night in a working men's club. The comedian, an ageing boozer with a frilled shirt and a Beatles wig, who has alternated dirty stories with gems from Italian opera throughout the night, has now taken the spherical mike in both hands, has closed his eyes, turned up his brows as though all set for the Garden of Gethsemane, and breathes the first lines of the crowning piece of the evening.

'When you walk through the storm hold your head up high . . .'

The mood changes. Older women shift in their seats and prepare themselves for a modest propriety . . .

'And don't be afraid of the dark . . .'

A moment ago those reverential lips were cracking out the absurdities of the arsehole. '—Yet another dose of Syrup of Figs. "Now," says the doctor, "'ave you been moved?" Patient says, "No, but something's bound to 'appen soon." Doctor sez, "Oh, tell me why, my good man." Patient sez, "Because this 'ere bed's full of shit."' Eyes recently streaming in laughter moisten again at the memory of some pretty stormy days of the economy.

'At the end of the storm is a golden sky
And the sweet silver song of the lark . . .'

His voice rises into a vibrato as he touches everybody's ancestral memory of the pastoral life, a life reduced now to lakeland mystery tours and hopes of heaven.

'Walk on through the wind.
Walk on through the rain
Though your dreams may be tossed and blown . . .'

And from the audience automatically rises that sound, possibly the most moving and pathetic in the world, of multiple voices rising like a vast unearthly ghost of solidarity and false optimism.

'Walk on' runs into one word, 'walkhon'. Half the men present sang the same song yesterday afternoon at the football ground. Eyes are visibly aswim. There is a careful seriousness around each table. This solidarity which we affirmed in our laughter is finally the most sacred thing we have. The songsmith might have been writing a hymn of avowal for lovers, or even just a hymn of religious faith, but its football usage has given it a different and weightier sense, so that when we all thunder 'You'll never walk alone' at football ground or club we are bestowing our loyalty on no individual but on the neighbourhood, the tribe as represented by its incarnate royal gods, its football team, and finally, sitting behind the seas of dirty glasses in the Sunday-night club, we are bestowing our loyalty on the entire class, on common folk, on the human condition, even on life itself.

This mystic communal love, which wins wars, burns Pakistanis, and stifles individuality, celebrates, within the family or the neighbourhood, a powerful mutual tolerance. The fatalism with which you travel each and every highway your way, finding losing amusing as tears subside, is so shared by family and neighbours that even though the careful step along the byway that you took your way, might lead you past Delilah's window to see the flickering shadows of love on her blind, and ultimately to stop her laughter with a knife, even this is only human. Who indeed could have taken any more? You did after all beg forgiveness before they came to break down the door, as indeed you later did what you did, not for yourself but for Maria. So as you dream surrounded by those old grey walls along with the guard and the sad old padre, you can be assured that in the vast beyond we'll all be waiting, Mary included, arms full of that green green grass of home, which isn't very green down Buttershaw Lane but it's home just the same.

Englebert Humperdinck, Tom Jones, and the sentimental guise of Elvis Presley, all owe their debt for these songs to a curious complexity of sources. 'The Green Green Grass Of Home' is almost straight country-and-western, being closely related to songs about faithful dogs and horses, but it also glances over to the mawkish ballads of the thirties like 'When I Grow Too Old To Dream' and 'I'm Walking Behind You On Your Wedding Day', and thence looks right back to the Victorian drawing-room ballad. A genteel tradition, at its most genteel in the ballads of Stephen Foster but pepped up and broadened for the people by music hall and minstrel shows in songs like 'She Was Only A Bird In A Gilded Cage' and 'That Old Fashioned Mother Of Mine', it extends to the mass of Edwardian Irish ballads — 'Smilin' Through' and 'Mother McCree', and the exquisite 'Danny Boy'. The road from the lyric peasant voice of John McCormack to Tom Jones and his personality of a well-matured Teddy-boy is marked out by Joseph Locke and Harry Secombe.

In Joseph Locke's repertoire a side road extends to the musical comedies of Richard Tauber. The musical comedy, however, avoided the bathos, pathos and sheer guts of the aesthetic with which we are concerned. Developing out of the exclusively bourgeois idiom of light opera, it travelled through 'Chu Chin Chow' and 'The Maid Of The Mountains', was passed by Jerome Kern, to Cole Porter, Gershwin and Rogers and Hart, who made high art of it.

From the personality of the romantic tenor comes the personality of the avuncular MC, and from the personality of the avuncular MC comes the personality of the avuncular DJ. Jimmy Young, whose platter-patter is deeply soaked in a reassuring domestic sentimentality, is perhaps the most highly developed of these. Max Bygraves has finished up in the same mode whilst Charlie Chester moved from comedy into his truly bizarre record programme wherein he features the poetry written and sent in by his listeners together with occasional pearls from his own hand.

The tear-jerkings and soul-wrenchings of Lulu, of Cilla Black, of Dusty Springfield, of veterans Dorothy Squires and Shirley Bassey, are all drawn from pop, movie-musical or Tamla Motown. Nevertheless in the throats of these lassies with the common touch the material merges with that of the male singers and goes howling over the footlights with the same effect.

The separate traditions of the material are merged most completely, however, in Yorkshire TV's *Stars on Sunday* programme, which expresses to perfection the moderation by the lower middle class of sentimentality, in a 'bit of good stuff', meaning material of subtlety and taste. Here is music hall represented by Gracie Fields, Harry Secombe and Dick Emery, with pop represented by the unbelievable Lovelace Watkins besides illuminati already mentioned, together with musical comedy and drawing-room ballad and popular hymns represented by a string of unremarkable tenors and sopranos, all of them heirs to the old Anne Zeigler/ Webster Booth act, and finally nonconformist chapel music of extraordinarily high quality performed by a number of highly capable choirs and brass bands. Dick Emery, the Midlands drag comic, rendering 'No Rose In All The World' perfectly in his perilously balanced voice, was a cultural cocktail not to be missed.

*Stars on Sunday* is cosy. Its loyalties are geared to certain securities. No one in those carefully illuminated chapels would forgive a crime of passion or wait on the Other Side for a jailbird. It is front-room stuff, at the Fifth Stage of social escalation. Respectable stuff. It represents with fantastic accuracy that point where the maximum conflict is, where the bottom-most rung of the middle class look out of their bay-windows at that topmost rung of the working class from whence the would-be respectable and the would-be cultured are clamouring to get in. That this is an area of conflict is quickly seen when one notes that this is the land of prints of the Annigoni Royal portrait and plaster busts of Churchill. This is the land of Protestantism in the full and loaded sense. These are the people who would say, along with the outlandish Ulster loyalist: 'I am British. My allegiance is not to the British government. It is to the British crown.' And these people are, of course, on Sundays anyway, *teetotal*.

If the present catastrophe in Northern Ireland is set against the traditional rivalry between Catholic Liverpool from the Scotland Road district, and Protestant Everton, each with their respective football teams (Heard on the Kop. 'Ye're weak as wee-wee, Everton.') or against the same situation in Glasgow with Catholic Celtic and Protestant Rangers (Two lads outside Celtic ground. One whips out his blade and cuts off the end of the other's nose. 'Whit d'ye du that for, Jimma?' 'It wis turnin' blu.' 'Oh Gee, thanks.'), this cultural demarcation becomes clear and it is surely this which is closer to the heart of the violence than anything to do with Canterbury or Rome.

So-called Catholicism has the self-defensive ethic of the slum. Its special aspiration is towards greater pleasure and greater privilege. The Protestant aspiration is towards the demonstration of conspicuous and competitive moral superiority. Catholics are 'no better than they should be'. Protestants all feel that they should be better than they are. The loyalty and fatalism of 'You'll Never Walk Alone' could be said to represent a more Catholic mood whilst the aspiration towards a real cultural emasculation in, say, the musical pilgrimage of John Hanson, expresses just that yearning not only for respectability but also for those far-off Edwardian days when the middle class was triumphant that constitutes the Protestant ethic.

Thus the gilt and curdling shades of crimson, emerald and pig-pink in cheap

Catholic ornaments, in plaster madonnas, holy water troughs, wall-hangings, crucifixes, bleed the pain and aggressive sensationalism that fill rich ditches of sentimentality. Catholic ornament retains something of the brash glamour of the Second Stage carnival, as though it were designed for tinkers and horse-dealers. The crotcheted homilies of Patience Strong avoid both pain and passion at all costs unless they are bestowed upon the kingdom of small animals and the sinister world of foreigners: 'But many migrants as they cross the continental lands/are shot before they get to Britain, snared by cruel hands/barbarous and inhumane, they slaughter in their flight/the little choristers of God that sing for man's delight.'

*Woman* magazine with its suburban ethic fans the flames of marriage expectancy and domestic efficiency along with *Woman's Own, Home and Beauty* and the distinguished *Lady's Journal*. 'A telephone rang beyond a wall; a radio was turned on somewhere in the distance, but she didn't hear anything. It was as if a tide were rising slowly inside her, warm, sweet, growing stronger and stronger until suddenly, as the quiet, floating moments passed, she didn't feel flat-footed or heavy or ungainly any more. She felt the most beautiful girl in the world.' 'Do be firm on yourself because all this is very unfair on your husband. I'm all for husbands lending a hand when they can, but after his day's work a man deserves a decent meal and a pleasant atmosphere. . . .' '"And you didn't need—" I began, astonished, but his lips stifled my voice. His arms were about me. As always between us there was no need for words. All we needed was each other.' 'Your parents don't make restrictions just to spoil your fun, but because they love you and want to do what is best for you in the long run.'

The flames of more passionate sexual sentimentality are fanned by magazines like *Secret Story, Real Romance* and *True Life Confessions*. 'Dear God, how could this be happening? I hadn't slept with anyone but Dave, yet now I was pregnant . . . he looked at me with hate and said, "YOU'RE NOT HAVING MY BABY . . . I'M STERILE!"' 'MY WIFE . . . MY EX-MISTRESS . . . MY ILLEGITIMATE SON . . . We Were All Living In The Same House.' 'STRIPPED AND RAPED' . . . 'At times, of course, I hungered for Tim — physically hungered for him. . . .'

It is no accident surely that the sharp-breasted girls in these magazines, caught as they are in typical situations of gutsy romantic pain as they watch their mothers seduce their lovers and adapt to paralysed husbands, as they find their way to contraception and the heat attending this forbidden subject, along with the discovery, by Editor's advice, of the clitoris, no accident that they look wildly towards mirrors, windows and opening doors with the tears of crucifixion. The whores who fall in love, or the erring wives who are forgiven, take on the lineaments of Mary Magdalene, if they narrowly miss the halo. None of them would be

*"See on the breast of the ocean*

*Skerry and island gleam,*

*Tinged with the crimson of sunset,*

*Lovely and strange as a dream."*

welcome at home with Evelyn Home, or even with Fanny Craddock.

The nobility of these perverse and randy saints, with their long legs, tight skirts and torn blouses, is one marked by shock, pain and violence. They are passionate martyrs motivated finally by love, loyalty, by sexual appetite. What is missing is the long-suffering sense of duty and propriety which guides the heroines of Ivy Preston, Rona Randall, Ivy Ferrari and numerous others, as they sacrifice their way through situations of pride and self-effacement in *Woman's Weekly Library*. This pocket-size paperback series, along with its parent magazine and the newsprint, two-colour-cover *Red Letter*, *Family Star*, and *Secrets*, continues in the low-church Protestant tradition of *Peg's Paper*. Puritanical and idealist in the older, homelier fashion, this is the literature of the wayward daughter's virgin, stay-at-home, parentally-favoured sister. It expresses an idealism that has already half spent itself in chapel bazaars and sitting with the aged.

It could be said, then, that the sentimentality that is sweetened by martyrdom is a mode that has almost surpassed sentimentality. It merely remains sentimental because the glossy wounds of gaudiness in the religious decoration conquer disaster as do the ennobling tears of the raped. The hard culs-de-sac of death and sexual compulsion are still denied. Faith holds fast. Driven by foul impulses, surrounded by the bombed and shattered, something comes shining through called love, or life, or fate, or God, or goodness, or something that disarms disaster and protects us in a cocoon of inevitable triumph.

The baldest manifesto for the faith which has been handed down from David Whitfield to Presley and Jones is the liturgical 'I Believe'.

As this never-to-be-forgotten anthem rises from the multiple larynx in club, pub, or charabanc, it argues that the positive result exceeds the negative initial event throughout nature. For every drop of rain that falls a flower grows, we maintain, whilst there's always a candle glowing in the darkest night as a matter of course. There is a natural law of balance which summons someone to show the way every time anyone goes astray. We believe, we cry, and then we cry it again. We believe that someone in the great somewhere is around listening to smallest prayers. Of all this we are certain from such conclusive evidence as hearing new-born babies cry, touching leaves and looking at the sky. As a result of these experiences we believe.

This song is perhaps best heard as sung by meths drinkers on an East End bomb-site. Lost exiles from the Northern cities, most of them, they crouch desolate in the metropolis, severed from class, neighbourhood, family, church and chapel, but none the less recreating the security they remember of their homes with this extraordinary song. The poignant fallibility of this vast faith is made no less painfully ironic by one's believing every contention of the song oneself.

# NOAH'S ARK

The story of the Flood, the saving of the innocent animals by Noah and his amazing Ark, the concept of an all-seeing, all-creating God behaving like a perplexed landlord expelling the gypsies from his policies, is generally conceded, even by those of the Christian Faith, to be probably untrue. Attempts to explain the origins of the Universe, the Earth, the Animal Kingdom in all its diversity, and Man himself, in non-historical terms are generally discredited and the results regarded as simple Non-sense. However, Nonsense, in order to be funny, demands a fair measure of feeling for Sense, verifiable evidence of the rational order of the physical world — Nonsense emphasises the evolutionary, historical character of Nature by deliberately breaking its rules. As is constantly being proved, Man's imagination is no match for the real complexities of the Universe. The more we learn of the past, the more we stretch Geological time, then the more we see that compression is one of the major distorting factors.

The elaborate reconstruction of Noah's Ark at Blackpool Pleasure Beach con-cedes the non-truth of the tale and presents it, in desperate detail, as reassuring testimony to the foolishness of pre-scientific Man, enslaved in myth and superstition. We are free, rational, triumphantly human, devoid of fear, inhabitants of the Modern World. However, this is not a simple painstaking reconstruction of an ancient fable, a piece of childish nose-thumbing at fundamentalist beliefs. It is a bit of daftness. Banished is the dove of peace, that discredited symbol of Armistice. Instead we have Radar to spy out the first signs of re-emerging land. Television is now added to the shipboard equipment — what home is complete without one? This Ark has set sail from Suburbia bearing its cultural heritage in its every line. It is the triumph of the civilising architecture of the garden hut, the self-erected garage. Tulips from Amsterdam crowd the flat-dwellers' windows. The chimney is askew, to suggest haste — or incompetence or amateurism as attributes of innocence and goodness. The roof-ridge dips in Disneyesque folksy manner to denote oldness. The World is compressed to a few square miles, the continents squeezed into a town-map with a handy zoo to facilitate collection, and of course a couple of immigrant communities from which to snatch a representative of our less-favoured coloured brothers to add to the collection of fauna. This footnote to History, the provision of a rational detail to an irrational story — the ancestor of the African People in the form of a stagey clownish 'darkie', as lovable as a pet dog, a cruel parody of the plantation 'nigger', his goggle eyes and inane grin, his labourer's stripes, denoting his station as a sub-species, the impassive long-suffering 'coolie' with his comical clothes, the oriental of Raffles rather than Mao — is basic British Empire of the *Rover,* the *Wizard* and the *Boy's Own Book of Heroes and VC's.* Noah, with deerstalker and gaiters, is a Shavian patriarch, standing guard by his Belisha beacon, preventing the dinosaur from boarding. And, no doubt, the Phoenix, the Great Yak, the Kraken, the Unicorn and the Sphinx have their absence explained by their exclusion. Why is the saurian excluded and sentenced to extinction? They are shown to be a failed experiment, superseded by the warm-blooded, cuddly animals, whose common fundamental nature is asserted, whose plurality of forms is dismissed as vestmentary, denying their evolution and their essential natures, rather than highly evolved and successful adaptations to their different environments. They are represented here as grotesques, without meaning or sense, as part of the concept of Man as the hub of the Universe, who can despoil or preserve the World as he wishes. The World as his Property, to be exploited, sold up, developed or squandered as he decides is implicit in this presentation.

Noah is an Englishman. He has saved the Natural World, converted it into Property, given a new value to each and every thing in it, so that all things in Nature can be expropriated by those who have the purchasing power to ransack it. The whole of Nature becomes one with Man's contrivancies, a subject for a television programme, a new use for Wild Life which will permit and justify its continued existence. What use would T. Rex's teeth be against a small boy armed with a rocket launcher. Dinosaurs were losers. Like bronze medallists, they dared to compete and must suffer the consequences of competition, oblivion. This Ark is seen, not as the instrument of Divine benevolence conferring a second chance on Humanity, to curb Man's arrogant assumption of divine power: this Noah *is* Jehovah. Man is the Master of the ship, the entrepreneur, the Merchant Prince, the Ruler of a materialist single society with a global policy of acquisition. The simple tale of the 'Great Flood', where a local disaster encompassed all the 'known' World and was transformed into a poetic image, is divested of its poetry and is deprived of meaning.

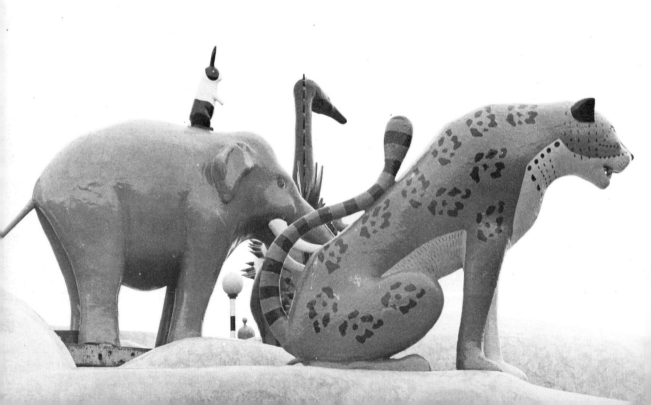

# YANK

Tracing the strains of church and chapel, music hall and cinema, slum and suburb, kitchen sink and front room, in this pungent melting pot, it becomes increasingly clear that whatever powers we bring to bear on our transmutation of material into our own cultural language much of the material we transmute is pure Yank. Jazz, swing, review, burlesque, rock-and-roll, Hollywood movies, pin-ups, fairgrounds, milk-shakes, jukeboxes, pin-tables, fizzy pop, canned beer, are all components of the culture of chrome and flash and big brash muscle-flexing noises that started to pour over the world after the '14–18 war.

Ever since the Original Dixieland Jass Band played Hammersmith Palais the routine has been that the West End jet-set pick it up, London fashion promoters sell it and the working class buy it and adapt it so that the yawning difference between Las Vegas and Butlin's can be clearly seen.

For the American mode is always hip, denies domesticity all along the line, has no conceivable connections with class loyalties and is in fact the language of the itinerant worker's fast fuck rather than of the predatory half-nelsons of the English working-class mating rituals. In fact the working-class attitude to the implied promiscuity of the jazz culture is defined by very typical contradictions.

Elvis Presley, or Mae West, or Tallulah Bankhead, may symbolise an orgy of permissiveness that is nearer home. They are, after all, a far cry from those who claim sexual freedom as an aristocratic birthright; but on the other hand when

they come too close, as Proby did that night at the working men's club, then delirious hostilities spring up and intoxicating poisons start to flow. The women flock hysterically to the US air base, disgusting even the GIs themselves with their shrill, acquisitive nymphomania. The men brood, mutter, brew powerful hatreds and when it's safe to strike, maim and murder, for the brash, loud, colourful boastfulness of the jazz mode is precisely the mode that will never be tolerated in English industrial cities. Self-exaltation amongst the mass breaks the deepest and the most powerful of taboos. The English North is a place where a man can have his face kicked in for the brightness of his tie. The fact that this is not so in the West End of London is one of the chief factors that modifies the density of vulgarity in metropolitan life. London has become, along with any other metropolis, a community of refugees. People flock to London to escape the neighbourhood and the family. They want to be cosmopolitan. They want the speed, freedom and flattering glamour that goes with a separate identity. They want to be hip.

Consequently whatever neighbourhoods and family groups they form will be loose-knit. There will be nothing like such a severe need for the devices of double-standard and taboo that hold good in the North. The comedians will tell sick jokes. It is significant that Mike Reid can take the twitches and stutters of the brain-damaged pill-head as his stage style. Nudity and straight pornography will thrive openly. A working-class audience will take all the four-letter words without a tremor. Petty crime is an integral and traditional part of the fabric of working-class life. Sexual infidelity is carried on with less tension and less secrecy. The accurate *mores* of *Sparrers Can't Sing* is something foreign to the North. London prostitutes are more plentiful and are usually very beautiful. People are fast-thinking, competitive, suspicious of one another, wry, sardonic and smart. In London, then, the American jazz tradition, its forms and behaviour, translates so easily as to be scarcely a translation at all. Even the transatlantic accents sound natural when compared with those more-stilted provincial attempts that surround the American air bases. It was out of this metropolitan transatlanticism that the teenage-rebel culture sprang with its complete rejection of family, class, middle age, work ethic, sexual hypocrisy, and European entertainers, with its emphasis on those qualities most detested amongst the British working class, vanity, idleness and effeminacy. The teenage movement never completed itself in the North as any thirty-year-old miner will tell you in his Iti suit, with his slim-jim tie and his DA haircut, as Paul McCartney will show you if set next to Mick Jagger.

So how the thing that started somewhere between New Orleans, Coney Island and Hollywood gets to Blackpool and Southend is a story of subtle changes. What there is behind the sound of the Original Dixieland Jass Band that becomes visible in the organ of the Granada, Tooting, or the Odeon, Birmingham, what makes the

jangling of ragtime and boogie-woogie so very like the sound of the jackpot falling from a fruit machine, and why a swing-band trombone section and the klaxon of a Buick both sound like a train whistle moaning over the Chicago stockyards, has to do with a sense of perpetual swaggart mobility that is ultimately hostile to working-class life, because it knows no roots and enjoys no clearly defined aims, a mobility that necessitates a sexuality that is superficial, promiscuous, dynamic and anti-domestic.

Thus the perception of the utterly crude colouring and drawing in those curious scenes illustrated on the upright sections of pin-tables becomes in Britain one of a kind of perverse revenge. The rawness of the pin-table arcade attracts people who want to tear to fragments the more stately forms and colours of their class inheritance. Whilst the South Seas jungle flowers across the front room and the black-lace pantee-girdle reinforces the deadlock of marriage, the violence and brashness of pin-table colours, of dodgems and chairoplanes with their super-powered amplifiers and speed, shatter if only temporarily the anxieties related to family security and the long, slow climb towards social status.

The chromium of the cars along with the chromium of the Pleasure Beach flashes so violently it creates a watershed of temporary anarchy before the pitched battles of home and class are again resumed.

The fundamental sado-masochism of jazz with its howls and squeals and roars of sexual arrogance is a mood to express a temporary anger against the sheer tensions and aspirations of working life.

But the actual music called jazz and blues which lies behind 90 per cent of popular music in this century is finally the high art of the vulgar, the standing proof that vulgarity *is not the absence of sensibility but is an aesthetic in its own right with possibilities at least as great as those of the finest taste.* Jazz takes the unmentionables that music hall had toyed with, which were, in any case, by no means so unmentionable in American negro vaudeville, the qualities and attitudes that the governing class can never truly tolerate, and howls them angrily to such a pitch that jazz, along with the aesthetic behind the best recent art, creates a skill and an eloquence of the vulgar sensibility that surpasses the finest levels of good taste. It is the real spearhead of cultural revenge. It is therefore bound to be embraced in some development or other by the working class all over the world.

No English source could have openly expressed the extremes of passion and blood that are ennobled in jazz but perhaps more clearly expressed in the proliferation of popular pain in American joke shops, in American weapon lore, in horror comics and horror movies, in the pictures and stories of the cheaper American men's magazines.

Cruder and vastly more disgusting developments from the old 10c pulp magazines, *Thrilling Detective*, *Black Mask* and so on, *Men in Adventure*, *Man's World*, *Man's Epic* and a whole string of others, throw butchery and breast together in vile juxtaposition and the rawest of three-colour reproduction.

The purpose of the supposedly true narratives in these magazines is to legitimise violence. The men are the comic-book, big-chest, square-jaw Rock Hudson character. The girls are suffering victims carried out of their slightly more domestic martyrdom in *True Life Secrets* and set in Stalag 13, in which heightened situation their bras and suspenders are brutally revealed by guard dogs as the blood trickles down their shackled wrists. The shackling is done by a couple of Texans in Gestapo uniform while the guard dogs strain at a leash held fast by the victims' identical sister in smart black shirt and swastika armband. Meanwhile GI Joe, manly as ever, is coming to the rescue through the underbush. The revenge of rape is in

# "TONIGHT WE HIT FEMALE TORTURE STALAG 13"

Our blood froze when we heard the shrill screams of mindless horror. We went kill-crazy with our hate.

By BILL DODD
as told to
STEVE BENSON

THE tow line's been cut. Up ahead the big mother plane banks at 45 degrees and turns back towards Dover. A gust of wind catches our plywood glider.

I look at my chronometer. The dial winks back at me. It's 2100 hours. In two minutes we should ditch within three kilometers of Givet.

I've never heard of Givet, but that isn't surprising. It's 6 July, 1944 and there's a lot about France that we don't know. It's going to be a good six months before every schoolboy will be able to tell you that Givet's only a spit and a holler from Bastogne.

Lt. O'Hallihan fingers his rosary. He sees me studying him and gives me a tight lipped grin. I check my wire-cutters and stare down at my *(Continued on page 50)*

"Get the dirty bastards!" I shouted at them

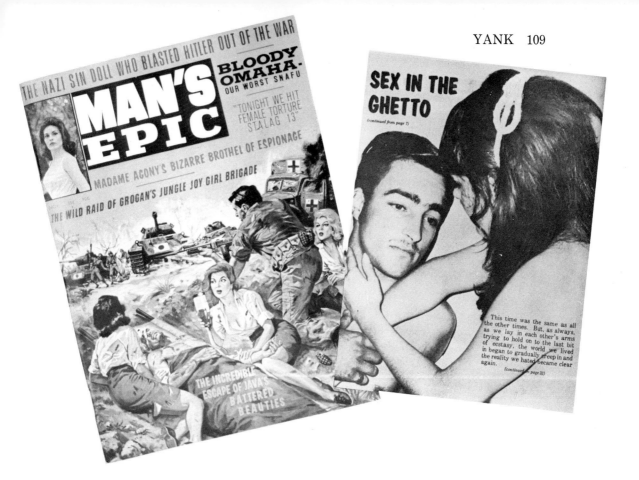

fact the simplest and most common ticket into blood-orgy. Hell's Angels, Jap guards, Nazis, Mafia, all fall either to the rescuing hero or to the girls themselves who occasionally whip through hordes of ecstatic males, fingernails ripping and tommy-guns blazing.

On the cover of *Man's Epic* girls with their uniforms designed for a burlesque chorus crouch on their thoroughbred thighs in the trenches, pumping blood transfusions into the orgasmic wounded. The umbrella of noble intentions and moral licence is intact throughout. Only in the ads are direct appeals made to queers who want satin jock-straps or wankers who want hard porn. The parallel between patriotism and sexual repression is so clear it becomes ludicrous.

But sublimation is by no means the whole story of this curious buzz that sounds close to the heat of the jazz aesthetic. The tongue with the nail through it, the joke hatchet that attaches to the head, the rubber doll stamped 'Born Dead', lead back to Little Audrey stories and Mark Twain's subtle hysteria.

It is the contrived heightening of the aesthetic in order to achieve energy. It is different from English popular culture in that its purpose is not to survive by the maintenance of lowest common denominators that act as a kind of community cement; its purpose is not to survive at all in fact, but to win. It is a machine to produce competitive energy and carries with it the awareness that an American, if he is to be the 'man' in all these magazine titles, must achieve the cruelty along with the panache necessary to make it to the top. The mood is the arse-end of the American dream which, being perverse, perversely grew into jazz, the highest unique achievement of Americans, achieved by blacks because their colour prevented them from rising to the more completely sublimated regions in this sordidly transcendental political torso.

The sharper, dourer quality comes when the English version, by juxtaposition, transforms the mood. You sit in a cinema watching a Mickey Spillane movie. Dashiell Hammett stated it with his brilliant blood baths, contrived, like the men's mags, in the name of Uncle Sam. He sold it to *Black Mask* and it came down through the pulp mags to the current sado-masochistic journals. Chandler's Phil Marlowe. Gardner's Perry Mason. Dick Tracy. Rip Kirby. Hank Janson. Humphrey Bogart. Peter Cheyney's Lemmie Caution. James Hadley Chase. Jack Webb in Dragnet. Elliot Ness. And Mike Hammer. The situations are these. Girl betrays hero after crass seduction. (Janson: 'She walked towards the bed and lay down next to me. Her face was expressionless, remote even.') Hero gets beaten up. (Chandler: 'There was a sudden pool of darkness at my feet. I dived into it.') Hero gets drunk — he is anyway alcoholic. Hero finds a number of corpses in tersely described living rooms. (Hammett: 'But that was all except a blue cotton sleeve in the middle of the floor, a straw sandal near the passageway door, and a handful of black hairs, a bit blood-smeared, beside the sandal.') Finally, hero reveals all, to the remaining unmurdered cast, in a room with a French window.

Mike Hammer, though, is in the dame-slapping situation. It is as formal and stylised as a Western. The crack of his palm. The Mary Magdalene bowing of the girl's head, the fall of the blonde bang to shroud her humiliation and shame. The close-up of blood on her already well-painted lips. Then the bag of sweets rustles behind you and that is all that's needed to change the meaning of the whole ritual.

The Big Dipper, with its New York police siren and its ragtime caricature of a Bronx elevated railway, hurtles down its slopes like a bullet. The boy who collects the money stands on the rear car, chewing nonchalantly, tipping his body perfectly to the pull of the car. He is hip and sharp and free and is contriving the image to express it. He is a cowboy. A GI. A gangster. And as the cars rattle down their precipices a shriek goes up from the forty female throats that somehow betrays the conductor's image of himself. Once more the situation has been transformed.

The Hank Janson novel lies on the kitchen table next to the knitting.

The ted lounges in the dock wearing his sneer. 'He's a good, good boy when he's not in the drink,' says his Irish mother.

A Mecca dance band is playing 'A-Train'. One of the saxophonists is given to grimaces and shoulder-hunching. Behind his back the others smirk.

The trumpets and trombones were trained with Brighouse and Rastrick Brass Band and sound like it. Precise and *conscientious*.

A demolition-worker drives a tipper at some speed on to the site. ''Oo the fuck d'yer think you are? Elliot Ness?' asks the foreman.

The structures are still there. Family and job. Dream if you must but don't get above yourself.

A Bradford cop shoves a Bradford hippie into the Black Maria. 'Come on, Charles Manson,' he says.

'Wur are we goin'?' asks the boy in broad Yorkshire. 'California?'

# TOYS

The twentieth century invented childhood. The concept of the child inhabiting a separate world from adults is a relatively new one. As far as the toy manufacturer is concerned, to judge from his products, it is a concept which finds no favour. The majority of toys one sees in the shops are scaled-down copies of objects of everyday use, as if the only difference between man and boy, woman and child, was one of size. Indeed it is the speed with which children assume adult mannerisms and attitudes that is one of the demarcation lines between the working class and the middle class. There are a few toys on the British toy market which are designed to allow the child a role in his play activity which transcend the limitations of the toy and allow his imagination to take over. This imaginative world is closed to the adult. The best we can do is acknowledge it. Because we endow all human objects with meaning, this meaning overcomes all its other potential. The child has no such restrictions. Objects have form, they exist in terms of his sense apparatus, so that he can experience them. To acknowledge and foster this requires a sacrifice on the part of the adult, to change his role of parent, of representative of the adult world, its scale and values, to one of observer.

Toys are fairly expensive. The requirements of children are very often the last thing to be considered in their purchase. The toy manufacturer is aware that the child has no purchasing power, so the market is directed at the point of sale. Most

toys, then, reflect the categorised activities of modern life. The myths of political life are expressed through guns. Curiously, the exception to up-to-dateness is in the production of hand guns of the nineteenth century, the six-shooter with the fire power of a machine gun. These antiques live happily side by side with reproductions of the most advanced weapons because TV and the cinema have endowed them with magical powers — they never, in the right hands, miss. They never apparently require re-loading or cleaning. How often has one watched the scene in the Western movie when the bad guy, with the hero at his mercy, realises that his pistol is no longer spitting lead? He throws it aside in disgust, his trust in modern technology betrayed at the vital moment. The hero *never* throws his gun away: he has too much respect for the industry which produced it, he is aware of its meaning — it won the West — and lastly one doesn't throw aside a valuable piece of property. This shiny representative of the great myth of the expansion of industrial society, the myth of progress spreading westwards from Europe, has possessed every child in the Western world.

The mass-production of toys has given industrial societies a valuable educational aid. It familiarises the child with all the things adults accept as normal: war and the death of young men, speed, motor cars and jet-planes, science and space-travel, the upbringing of babies and the domestic role of women, sport and winning, etc.

The miniaturisation process is at times anomalous. While 'toy' means to make small, many toys can retain, like the hand guns, their scale, and are in effect reproductions of the real object in all save one important feature — function. Because of the literal structure of the adult world we forget that many human objects do not externalise their function. Their appearance can be made to carry any reference, however unrelated. The toy, then, can be made associative in a social sense in relating the technological or functional origin of the object which has given rise to its appearance and which may be frightening or threatening, with domestic animals.

There is a whole bestiary, transforming machines into benevolent beings. The adult world tends to obscure the brutal and bloody effects of the development of machines, the destructive power, the scale of slaughter on the world's roads, the erosion of the land, the quarrying, blasting, gouging in pursuit of minerals, the stink, smoke and filth of the cities and the pollution of the atmosphere. Society continues to believe, against all the proof to the contrary, in the power of machines to produce a benevolent and healthy world. So the brutes are humanised, diminished, given a stereotyped avuncularity, assume the mythical goodness of the machine. Railway engines become choo-choos; motor cars become brrmm-brrmms. This concession to infancy suggests the condition is akin to mental deficiency, the logical outcome of assuming children to be incompetent adults.

Many toys simply function by extolling the manufacturing processes which produced them. They are testimonials to the ingenuity of machines, the clever accomplishments of cutting, bending and fastening. 'Tin toys' particularly have this quality, of being in fact quite different from the real objects they represent by virtue of the way they are stitched together, the extraordinary quality of the print-on of the iconographic elements of appearance, the strange blend of two-dimensional and three-dimensional information, the practical 'play' elements of the reality of the toy and the illusory socialised clues to the meaning of the model. Die-cast toys are true microcosms of the real adult world. The external appearance of the popular mass-produced car is almost entirely governed by social myths. The appearance is pristine, jewel-like. They exude an air of speed, comfort and luxury — since they don't have to go at very high speeds they must appear to be fast while at rest — in contrast to real racing cars which look like fragile insects when at rest. The quality of the toy cars is truly astounding. Like complex costume jewellery, all the information about their selves has a hard, resistant reality. The paint finish is applied in the same manner, is the same colour and so functions in the same way. Its preciousness is enhanced by the use of faceted diamond-like gems set in as headlights. They glisten and shine, pure and hard, resistant to any attempts by the child to change their nature. Like the adult, the child can only own it as a possession. He is the owner, the licence holder, not the creator.

The child can fight back. He can employ in his play the natural world. He can endow twigs and sticks, stones, clay, water, grass, string, rubbish, throw-aways, the detritus of life which has been de-mythologised in the discard, with new meaning. He can perform without effort the alchemy of the mind, discover the world in the smooth touch of driftwood. A nameless world from a pile of sand. He creates life which has a greater history than the brief-lived, rigid, socialised objects which are thrust into his hands to reward him, console him or divert him, to trap him in the 'real world', where he must learn to excuse, possess and destroy.

# DOLLS

The doll is a true toy. That is, it is a shrunken reality. There are many toys which are representations of the human form, but they are carefully categorised by name — puppets — soldiers — models — Action Men. Dolls, or dollies, are part of the world of women, they are the little girl's entry into motherhood and domesticity. Two distinct kinds of doll exist: the baby doll, 'the dolly', and the mature girl doll. The latter group covers a wide age-group, representing all stages of growth from five to sixteen, the magic age.

The baby dolly casts the child in the role of mother. She cannot identify with the doll. She tends it, administers to it. It prepares her for a future life of service; to suppress her own needs; to bear the cost of her own sexuality. The concept of family unity is re-enforced, the little girl is taught to eschew the technology of the world which enforces change and disruption and concern herself with the 'real' world of the Home. The dolly is sexless. The lack of external genitals does not extol its femininity. Otherwise the doll is physically, fully expressed. It is not part of the adult world. Devoid of speech, free movement, control over its body, it can express no social meaning. The functionings of its body are as lacking in significance as a dog lifting its leg against a tree. The humanity of babies was expressed and acknowledged in these toys, long before it could be permitted to appear in representations of older children. Like all mass-produced toys they combine, in their complex structures, different kinds of reality. The morphology of machines and humans is mixed. It allows a distance between a total realism of human imagery which would be unable to overcome the stillness, and rigidity, the death-like immobility of the dummy.

So the joints are mechanical, the limbs detached, capable only of helpless gestures of supplication. So inert are these androgynous creatures, so devoid of wonder and joy, that mechanical contrivances are added to offer some semblance of participation. By means of a simple counter-balance the eyes open and shut when the doll is picked up or laid down. This is accompanied by a reedy bleat sounding faintly like MAMA. Like all mechanistic equivalents of biological processes it seems clumsy and inept. There is no hair present on the head; it is represented by ridges and whorls concealing the bony structure of the skull. Although the doll can be dressed it does exist as a naked object in a natural sense. Only when it is clad can it assume a social meaning rather than a biological one.

The modern doll is unchanged from its Victorian predecessors in one important aspect: it must reflect current fashion in clothes. Middle-class parents, with small families, tend to buy dolls for their little girls to act as surrogate companions. Lacking a real sister, however, the child often substitutes the doll for herself. She stands back and observes herself, playing, eating, bathing, going to bed. This is re-enforced by dolls which can now talk. What an extraordinary picture they give of a child's life. This imaginary child is fractious, boastful and totally involved in the minutiae of everyday existence. A no-nonsense child, unimaginative and superficial. She is dressed in Party Clothes, unstained, flouncy — 'feminine' — a future home-maker. She already knows her role in a man's world. The little pronouncements she makes when her speaking mechanism is activated reveal her conditioning already to acknowledge that women must be attractive, helpless, dependent on men. She may be a nurse when she grows up but never a doctor; a secretary but never a managing director.

The speaking device is so devised that it has a random element which suggests a degree of wilfulness in the doll . . . 'I'm going to jump in a puddle.' 'Must I go to bed this minute?' 'But I washed my neck yesterday.' 'I want to play in the wain.' 'I refuse to eat my cabbage.' 'I don't want to go to school today.' 'I shall scream, EEK!' 'I always have the smallest helping.' 'Why can't I stay up all night?' 'I can write my name.' 'I've got lots of crayons!' 'I usually sit next to Jane.' 'I can't spell at all.' 'She says I'm always talking.' 'My teacher was cross today.' 'She's my best friend after you.' 'Painting's my favourite lesson.' 'Why is apple jam pink, not green?' 'A big one with lemon icing.' 'Please may I leave the table?' 'What sort of soup is this?' 'I'm hungry. Is tea ready?' 'What is marmalade made of?' 'Milk shakes are nice aren't they?' 'Oh it's hot. Quick, water.' 'Oh good, my favourite cake.' 'Tickle me, Mummy.' 'I like the taste of toothpaste.' 'I can count, one, two, three.' 'I hurt my head. Kiss it better.' 'I like to wear my party dress.' 'I'm sleepy. Night night, Mummy.' 'Shall I sing a song, Mummy?' 'Come closer, I want to whisper in your ear.'

The doll itself is 'dressed up'. The innocence of youth is acknowledged in the white, practical vest; the dress itself reflects her mother's taste. Muted colour, perhaps spots or a figuring of flowers, new-looking, a hair ribbon, socks and button shoes. Her mother signals her marital status by confining her body in slightly outmoded styles as though they lost their potency, their erotic overtones, through the passage of time. So the child and her doll wear clothes of stereotyped femininity, a generalised version of women's wear over the last two or three decades, defused by vague allusion to the taste and fashion of the immediate past, not old enough to be costume but with the de-personifying quality of a uniform. A singular contrast between doll and child is the cosmetising of the doll's face. By its nature the doll's face must assume a rigidity of appearance in spite of the moving eyes. It is upon this generalised appearance that the commercial success of the toy depends. An idealised face is created, somewhere between adult and child. The child has thrust upon her the perfected, adjusted, improved female image, long dark eyelashes emphasising the glance, the pert nose, the erogenous mouth, the pink, thrusting tongue between the perfect white teeth, seductive and alluring, emphasising her physical being, her body made object. So the young child grows to think of her naked face as unnatural, inexpressive, too hidden behind a mask of social conformity.

The child also sees the adult as privileged. She seeks these privileges as tokens of favour. She strives to be a good little adult, earning commendation and approval. In one respect the doll of today is different from the nineteenth-century counterpart, for in freeing the adult from the taboos of sexuality and nudity we allow the toy to refer to them.

The Victorians emphasised the chaste nature of their women by shrouding their

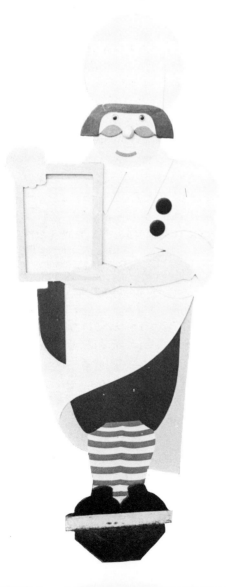

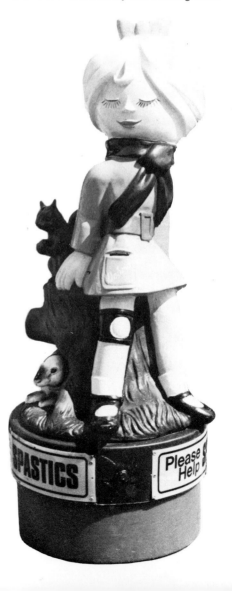

bodies in layers of garments, surrounding it with such mystery that it eroticised the *whole* body. Such was the ineffable power of the whole female body that the merest glimpse of an ankle was thought dangerous. The male became a constant voyeur, peering through the obscuring folds of cloth to discern the least betrayal of a human form beneath. This threw enormous demands on those parts of the body which were uncovered: the face and hands. We see this pattern reproduced in the doll of the period. The head made as realistic as possible, capable of the most detailed examination. The hair, long and uncut, caught up and moulded round the face, apparently soft and yielding yet firmly under control and defiant of gravity. It insists that the face is natural, naked and pure, concentrating social communication in eye contact and formal speech, in contrast to the rigid exoskeleton of her dress, which places it firmly in its social category. The tensions of such a schism are fully expressed by the construction of the doll, only the head, forearms and hands, lower legs and feet modelled in wax or porcelain, the rest a shapeless muslin bag, concealed beneath the real body, the dress.

There is a parallel in the toys made for young boys. Dolls play a negative role in their play, as a butt for their derision, an exercise in manliness. Boys' dolls are called toy soldiers. This instantly limits their use to exercises in the Martial Arts. Toy soldiers are always clearly marked with the signs of their historical context. We can identify their nationality by their helmets or battledress. They have a heightened reality, they are a microcosm of battle. Earlier toys paraded with ceremonial precision. Their red coats, cross belts, shakos, busbies and plumes turned each into a living object of State. They are small in scale, rigid in their cast construction but weighty and solid. Each proudly occupies a little square of green turf. This little piece of lawn signifies the formal field of battle, the professional armies meeting in open confrontation. The little boy does not identify with these unspeaking little pawns. He is the Marshal, the General, he commands the symmetry of their battle lines, their resolute advance, each with his gaze firmly to the front, their fear of death from the enemy nothing compared with the fearful discipline of their commander.

The mobility of modern war is expressed in the postures of toy soldiers of today. They refer almost totally to the Second World War. Many are now moulded from plastic. They are frozen in stills from newsreels, caught in mid-stride, they have submerged their propagandist images in ubiquitous plastic. All, whether Japanese, Russian, German, American or British, are equal, equally brave, equally caught up in some great competition. The plastic is slick and smooth, unscratchable. Each is permeated with colour, grey for German, ochre for Japanese, khaki for British and so on, approximating to the camouflage of their fatigues. The colour infuses their skin, only the shapes are left, their faces rigid in heroic earnestness. These troops are the people; when they fall, no splash of colour marks the spot, they merge into

the soil and their bodies melt and join with the earth.

And recently there has appeared at last the doll for boys. A true doll which, however, embodies an attitude rather than a role. The commando, the thinking soldier. The educated cynical killer. He is the product of modern war, the police action. The little homunculus is made with the machine precision of an automatic weapon. He operates with the same accuracy and efficiency. The child can identify with these toys. He can now play out the role of adventurer. The plots are ready-made, he cannot alter the rules of the game. He will not make any discovery, the dolls act on their own. The face of the doll shows dynamic energy. They all bear a scar on the left cheek. A duelling scar, perhaps, a mark of exclusiveness. The torso is that of an acrobat, a gymnast. The head is neat, almost square, the hair cropped, the features plebeian. He is the classless man, impatient of evolutionary change, despising politics and compromise. He is a weapon, unquestioning and unscrupulous. He is Action Man.

These toys are almost indestructible. They impart to the child a sense of invulnerability and nourish a desire for newness. But in these toys the newness persists, they do not lose their shininess, handling does not smooth out their already perfect surface. Although he changes his social role with each change of uniform or equipment, his essential nature resists. He is a challenge to authority, yet the child, in identifying with him, does not become a rebel. He merely learns another conformity.

# AUTOMATA

Automata have always had a simple appeal. First we are aware of them as mechanical contrivances — these are not the Androids of Sci-Fi. Even on a human scale they do not attempt to appear as 'real' people. The early eighteenth- and nineteenth-century models relied on the application of quite complex and advanced mechanisms, akin to the movements of clocks, to produce animation; and no doubt as great a wonder was derived from the harnessing of machines and mechanical power-sources in a governed and deliberate way, as the entertainment provided thereby.

Fairgrounds still provide us with the role of instant voyeurism. The human functions selected are common social acts. No Petomanic farts or Johnsonian belches, no manikin pissings or Rodinesque uncouplings are mechanically simulated for a penny. The figures employed are identified by their costumes as licensed and privileged performers, adding a new dimension to their apparently meaningless gestures and acts. Laughter assumes a maniacal frightening menace when it is not a response to an external stimulus. One automaton is dressed in costume, a clown's suit, a mock crown, seated on a throne, with a small figure — a pseudo doll — sharing the joke, their shrieks tinnily conveyed through a Tannoy, the figures protected from us by a glass window. Another clown jerks up and down, mimicking a puppet mimicking in its turn a clown dancing. In the spirit of the freak shows of the past, two toy babies lie helpless in a glass case. Like the headless lady, fed through tubes thrust down the truncated neck, they are attached to feeding bottles, endlessly competing with each other in vigorous suck.

# MOTORCAR

Nature conspires to return to the earth the very material of which the car is constructed. From the moment it is purchased the machine begins to deteriorate. Usage seems to speed this process; the motorcar seems to function best when stationary. The suburban motorist treats his car like a pampered thoroughbred horse, stabling it at night, rubbing down its shiny flanks and feeding its insatiable appetite. The paradox of the automobile is expressed in its outward appearance. It is the perfect object, first seen in these puzzling car sales rooms, trapped behind enormous windows, with no apparent door large enough to allow it passage — the locked-room puzzle of detection fiction. The pure glaze of its body colour, the mirrored chrome, the spotless tyres, deny any mundane origin. It expresses its hermetic nature in every line, it is the image of speed, of smooth passage through the air, the flow lines of which are inscribed in chrome on its sides. Within its domestic nature is asserted. It is fully furnished with fitted carpets and central heating, soft lights and music at the touch of a button.

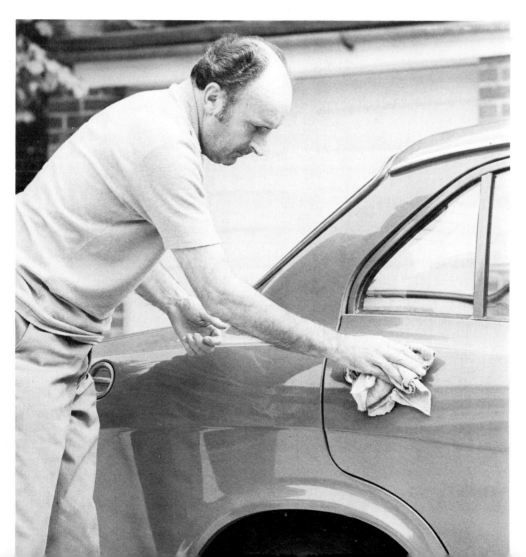

Since the beginning of the century the motorcar has caused more deaths and serious injury than all the weapons of war put together. Modern society rejects this unpalatable truth almost entirely. Speed kills, the car is implicated only through the failure of the driver, he must match the perfection of the machine or it will turn on him, impale him on the spike of its steering column, shred his skin with shards of glass and crush and break his bones with its unyielding metal. The fairy-tale magic carpet turns at the first sign of human fallibility into a ravening ogre, its victims already within its stomach, like uncaring Jonahs.

This conscious control of the machine is emphasised in the most pedestrian of mass-produced cars. Leather-covered, wood-rimmed, lightweight steering wheels imply that while every ounce of weight affects the performance of the car, the design team is deeply sensitive to the comfort of the driver, the decisiveness and skill required in the operation of 'Driving'. It is worthy of note that pilots of airliners are derisively called 'drivers' to imply the passivity of their role with the introduction of more and more sophisticated equipment in aircraft. In the car today the interior layout of the instruments resembles more the controls of an aeroplane; navigational

aids are optional but rev. counters, speedometers, oil temperature gauges, all reveal the inner workings of the hidden machinery. The car is equipped to cross the Sahara, to chart unknown territory. Driving is an adventure, the destination a mystery. To attain the dream of social advancement and all its attendant advantages, mobility and freedom, luxuriating on deserted Mediterranean beaches, beautiful women, expensive hotels and steak dinners, it is necessary only to purchase the car 'you have always promised yourself'. Only then will life become truly meaningful in the dreamworld that passes silently beyond the windows of the speeding vehicle and fills the enchanted windscreen.

# PRESS

If you talk to a group of people regularly you acquire certain techniques of intonation and stress. You choose your subject matter and diminish or extend it as required. You learn how much of the truth to tell and how much not to tell. You learn to say the things people want you to say. You learn to contradict and offend them only when they want to be contradicted or offended. You learn to gossip.

The English popular newspapers have perfected gossip.

The first rule in gossip is not to tell anything new. Novelty must be of the trivial, everyday kind. People are far more interested in births, marriages and deaths than they are in moon landings. They know all about birth, marriage and death and feel they can join in. They know nothing about moons except as an adjunct to copulation and engagement. You must talk about familiar subjects.

In popular papers the gossip is systematically sorted according to subject. Here are the categories:

1 The stupidity of the present government.
2 The truth which can 'now be told' about some past scandal, crime, government machination.
3 The stupidity of local councils and the scandals they persistently ignore.
4 The disgracefully low state of the morals of some lucky bastards; all the lovely things that ought to be stopped.
5 Noble-sacrifice or noble-suffering stories, close to the women's mags — 'In Constant Pain For Thirty Years' — 'Her Secret Sorrow'.
6 Royal Family stories, either hostile (left-wing Catholic) or friendly (right-wing Protestant). Either the awful cost or how lovely she looked.
7 Celebrity confessions. Linda Lovelace or Beverley Nichols tells all.
8 Personal reminiscences — How I met my husband/wife — My first ten confinements — The day our bomb dropped.
9 Intimate profile — What Barbara Windsor eats for breakfast. Also her favourite colour.
10 Ideal-mate stories — The story of the man/woman I did/should have met.
11 Home and Jesus columns — close to the sentimental ballad. Patience Strong in the *Sunday Mirror* was the master.
12 Medical-advice columns — sop to the hypochondriacs.
13 Personal-advice columns. Evelyn Home sedate to the end; and magnificent Marjorie Proops by far the best.
14 Horoscopes, along with other sops to the horse-players.
15 Short stories of two sorts. *Peg's Paper* sentimental and *Evening News* tough and snappy.
16 Violent news items, rapes, murders, road accidents. War news to be under-

played except in retrospect. It only makes good reading after we know we won. Arnhem and Dunkirk are now popular defeats.

17 Silly stories — The day grandma mistook a police box for a public urinal — The day dad put weedkiller on the prize roses.

18 Dialect pieces — particularly good ones in Yarmouth and Dudley.

The grandfather popular paper in England is the *Daily Mirror*, which was an American import and was the first paper to stress sensational news and human-interest stories in a banner-headline format. It was from the *Daily Mirror*'s example largely that newspapers began to look more like posters than stock-exchange lists because of the increasing emphasis on the selling headline. Other papers followed suit, notably the extinct *Daily Sketch* and the recent *Sun*. They developed typographical rhetoric. The overall effect of a popular newspaper layout is one of simple opinions shouted in a crowded situation. The blocks of type and the news shot make a patchwork of harsh dissonances and excitement. You feel that this is where things are being said and all the best tubs are being thumped.

The *Mirror* is the voice of the Old Codgers who run the Live Letters column. They are getting on but not past it, never shaken but sometimes justly angry, wry and endlessly knowledgeable. They are working-class patrist emblems. Doctors with council-estate practices, salesmen, landlords, politicians, all those whose function is to reassure folk, would do well to study them.

The *Mirror* has employed a number of towering great journalists like Cassandra, Noel Whitcomb, Keith Waterhouse, Donald Zec and Proops. They all have the *Mirror* skill of pinning their audience immediately. They are gossips of genius, good mates, good to drink with, no bores; the misery which Proops must have relieved is surely vast.

*Mirror* strips are archetypal — Buck Ryan, Garth, Jane. Just Jake and the Fosdyke Saga are considerable literature.

But the *Mirror* is a national paper and pays deference to a mixed class. Broadly vulgar though it may sometimes be, the finer notes of vulgarity are not really available in a paper of such tact and moderation.

The *News of the World* and the *Sunday People* seem to have a narrower target and have certainly become fine cooks of the sort of soup we are sniffing. The ritual remains of lamb fat and cabbage stalks amongst which these mixtures are imbibed into minds already heavy with the five or six pints that precede Sunday dinner, form a setting where the sexual tensions of the tight-knit family are seething and bubbling like indigestion. The weekly lethargic orgy that will take place about four o'clock in the front bedroom after the kids have been packed off out will be weighed down with carbohydrates on top of one weekend's boozing, and that on top of a week's hard work. Somewhere in this hampered coupling there will be the nurtured components of frustration, yearning for the dream orgy of the distant and the privileged, and the need to know that for all the sexual inadequacy decency has been preserved. We can watch the licentious by covering our envy in a sauce of moral self-righteousness. The *News of the World* and the *Sunday People* will cater for these appetites.

Susan George talking about her new love for Jack Jones, Alan's son, not the trade union leader (Remember 'Donkey Serenade', grandma?), says, 'I have just broken off a four-and-a-half year relationship that was like a marriage.'

The little bitch's got away with murder. What she wants is a couple of kids. And what about these two disgusting little cows who constitute the amazing love life of Mr Kiss. 'Some people will say we are sick or kinky,' says Laszlo under the picture in which he grins brutishly in bed, flanked by Pauline and Barbara. It's all very well for Sylvia and Rita who want to sell their babies ('My reasons are not just the money'). Mind you, *we* could do with the money and we did have to get wed a bit fast, but we clung on to ours. Let others sell their children and escape. We did the right thing.

The dream doctor who actually seems likely to provide the therapy every hypochondriac longs for comes to life in the person of Doctor Cauthery (name conveniently dovetails 'catheter' and 'cauterise'), partner of the monstrous Dr Cole, who has quite rightly been reported to the Medical Council. Says Alderman Anthony Beaumont-Dark, 'We do not want our children exposed to Dr Cole's views of life and people.' The informer, Dr Louise Eikhoff, such a sweet old lady, fills in some tasty details: 'Any police force knows of cases of strangulation brought about by the frustration of men who could not perform the sex-act properly.' Up the page, and slightly to the right Princess Anne straddles a stallion under the headline (in red) HOT TIP. 'What does a modern young princess say when she comes a right royal cropper off her horse? In the case of Princess Anne (that well-known sailor's daughter) it's something pretty fruity you may be sure.' Fancy that. She swears just like you and me. Isn't that nice? Disgusting really though, when you come to think of it. And just there, where the contradictions collide, that special buzz. The fusion of the righteous and the vicarious.

Mother got pregnant in 1958. *And* she got married. *And* had her baby. Not like these French girls coming over for abortions. No abortion clinics then. It says, 'Almost half of Britain's strippers have become pregnant and have had abortions on the National Health in the past year.'

There was Elvis then, though. A bloody sight better than Jimmy Savile ('Me And My 3,000 Birds'). 'Now then, how would any of you guys like to be locked up with Miss World for five months?'

Better than this load of poofs, too. 'Men For Sale. It's The Limit! Even In These Permissive Days' '—where will it all end? These are the kinds of imports, from Germany and elsewhere, that we could well have done without.' I wonder how much it costs to get over to Hamburg.

Until then maybe it would help if mother made a dummy like Barbara Nash, and like Barbara, kicked it out on the back lawn to relieve her tension — 'a shapely leg in a decidedly unladylike manoeuvre known as putting the boot in'. Or maybe become a female wrestler like 'petite, demure' Margaret Goodrum on page eleven.

Nothing petite, though, about '42-year-old granny Joan Butterwick' who offers sex for driving lessons. Fancy admitting that. Still, look at her. Bet it's the only way she can get it. At the bottom of the page another Abortion Clinic Shock. Revenge! Revenge! Unmask the bastards. Enoch is mentioned here and there. He'll sort 'em out when he comes to power. When we've had a good read about 'em (we have a right to know) and a good look at 'em (let's see what they look like) then he'll take care of the sex doctors, the abortion clinics, the baby-selling mothers, the roadside nymphomaniacs. He'll take care of Margaret Nolan who 'has no regrets' about the 'kinky pictures' she posed for before she got on TV with Jimmy Tarbuck and Des O'Connor. Enoch will avenge our weeping, itching envy that flows so sweetly after a week's fatigue or a couple of gallons of ale.

But still in these tabloids the obligation is towards the presentation of news. They remain defined as newspapers. The weekend popular magazines are relieved of this charade. Their pretence is to light entertainment and nothing else. The serious note is dropped. There is a holiday air. It's Saturday not Sunday. The moral scourge can be left behind.

Consequently the brew is less powerful, alleviated by colour and a general air of fun. An article about the magnetism of muscle-men in *Saturday Titbits* is headed 'MAGNIFICENT MEN ON THEIR TORTURE MACHINES' with a close-up of a bicep made into a hamburger with mustard, and oiled body-builders coiled in the early stages of oral sex. 'Oh the ecstasy of pain! Only the true bomber knows the feeling,' quotes the copy from its American sado-masochistic source. Then there's a blithe look at *'Tis Pity She's a Whore*, now a spaghetti movie. 'Life's no bed of roses when a girl goes too far with brotherly love.'

There's a different note. A delight in the scandal rather than a brooding. We all know we like a bit really and in a holiday mood we don't mind if it gets a bit pervy, maybe. Like Caroline and Susie who 'are always willing to do a favour' in the Sauna massage room. Because it's okay finally. The reason 'Why Men Really Get Married' is for security and companionship. And nude film actress Astrid Franks 'wants to be an actress who's clothed. At least most of the time.'

Even the sob story has a twist, like the tale of the woman who ran away. An anonymous corpse was buried in her grave, and now 'Every week a mother who came back from the dead makes a lonely journey — to where she was buried.' Get *Saturday Titbits* For That Saturday Feeling.

There's a bright showbiz complexion on *Weekend*. Barbara Murray and Thora Hird are 'Glad My Husband's A Nobody'. There's a quick run-down on torn-clothes girl-fights in Westerns. Steve McGarrett of *Hawaii Five-O* has a 'secret sorrow'.

*Parade* is a pin-up mag, but, along with *Titbits* and *Weekend*, it carries true-life adventures, mostly wartime stuff, snappy short stories, and police-file stories. The pin-ups in all these magazines are well-stacked, and ooze with allure, on their tiger-skin rugs, in their wet shirts and oriental drapes. There's a human-interest slant on many of them. The sex-therapy story that was disapproved in the *Sunday People* gets a merry write-up. There's a row of belly-dancing housewives from LA. And a sequence in the best *Spick·and Span* style of a young wife who finds it practical to strip on the decorator's ladder rather than get paint on her clothes.

The parent weekend mag is *Reveille*. *Titbits* was there first but the early *Titbits* was a mild Protestant affair until *Reveille* happened along. As its name implies it was aimed first at national servicemen, hence the pin-up emphasis. It's a quiet mag compared with its children, having all the components of the other mags without

the colour. It knows its public sufficiently well to keep breast and buttocks tautly covered at all times.

Not quite as well covered as they are in the *Weekly News*, though. Never has the masturbation market been so decorously catered for as by the *Weekly News* girls in their ample cardigans and their one-piece swimsuits. These pin-ups are prepared for a rather more respectable home than the one in which Sunday dinner takes place after the pubs shut and sex takes place when the roly-poly has settled. Opposite a corset ad with someone like the young Liz Taylor in something like a truss Michael Barratt chats about tomatoes in his chat column. Dick Emery reveals frankly that the 'TV sketch that brought scores of protests' was about killing a budgie. Sam Costa, sharply drawn by the house cartoonist, delivers readers' jokes up and down the pages. The human-interest stories never touch on sex. Most of them rely on a kind of 'who'd have thought it' tone, the answer being, in most cases, no one in their right mind. Items like 'Prisoner Sells Budgies On Visiting

# IT'S MARBELLOUS!

**A skilful thumb-all it takes to player into a**   **flick ... that's turn a marbles world champion**

CAN you imagine any man getting angry over a shapely girl showing an eyeful of thigh or cleavage? Well, the slightest sign of either is certain to start a rumpus this week when droves of dedicated fellows sink to their knees and do battle for the world marbles championship.

The event has been held every Good Friday at Tinsley Green, near Crawley, Sussex, for nearly 300 years. And if there's one thing the deadly serious competitors can't stand, it's the sight of female flesh.

They say they can't concentrate on rolling marbles when there are girls around wearing mini-skirts and plunging necklines.

Two years ago there was a rumpus when a group of girls tried to enter

**And here's world champion Len Smith (below) ... demonstrating his famous marble flick to a bevy of beauty**

the contest. The world marbles board branded the girls' mini skirts as undignified . . . and barred them.

The girls hit back with low-cut dresses and threatened to enter as a team, called Bosoms United.

One who got down to the serious business of marbles was 24-year-old Mrs Pam Winslet, of Crawley. "I don't think we put the men off at all," she said. "We are just adding a bit of glamour to the game."

World individual marbles champion, Len Smith, wasn't too concerned. "Bosoms and bottoms don't worry me," he said.

IN fact, marbles is one of the world's oldest games. Roman Emperor Augustus was a great enthusiast.

The annual contest at Tinsley Green dates back to when two local village lads vied for the hand of a lovely maiden.

After challenging each other to all sorts of sports, without either proving himself superior, it was decided to play marbles, with the girl as the prize for the winner.

Today's championship rules follow closely those which decided the girl's fate. Forty-nine marbles are put on a pitch, which is a ring of grass close to the Greyhound Inn.

Teams of six players take turns at trying to knock out a marble. By rule, only the thumb can be used to shoot a marble. A flick of the wrist is a foul and a contestant using it loses a round.

Each time a player knocks out a marble, he is entitled to another go. The team who knock out most marbles are the winners.

These days, interest in marbles is world-wide.

America has her own national championship, with a gold and velvet crown, a watch and a bicycle as prizes.

Some of the greatest fans are in Australia, South America, Malaya and Fiji.

In Britain, it is still one of the few sports untouched by commercial interests. There can be no financial consideration in the game at any time.

More than 60 countries buy British marbles. A century ago, clay marbles were the marbles. But today about 10 glass marbles are sold for every clay one and annual sales total about 100 million.

All that is needed for a game is a flat piece of ground and flicking the marbles can give hours of fun.

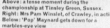

**Above: a tense moment during the championship at Tinsley Green, Sussex. Right: Mrs Pam Winslet, of Crawley, in action. Below: 'Pop' Maynard gets down for a marbles-eye view**

Day' and 'A Grandad Who Specialises In Skipping Wants To Take On Anyone In Britain In A Marathon Skipping Contest'. The series on 'How I Met My Mate' is warming to the heart only and lacking in the saucy details such a story would have had in *Weekend*. 'Hughie would come to meet me and we would go out from there. We went swimming quite often and for long walks.' The suffering stories were never nobler. 'Last Chance Operation Saved Our Little Boy — Her Own Story.' And the moral reprove is back — with no double standard but with a tut-tutting disapproval that precludes the possibility of vicarious envy. The letters are quietly domestic. There are no worries about bent husbands or infidelities. *Weekly News* readers don't have sexual problems, or if they do they keep them properly to themselves.

The reason why *Weekly News* is as safe and sound as Granny's cardie is that it is one of the national distribution products from Courier Place. Although published from the London and Manchester offices it carries with it all the impregnability and stern principle of that Chateau d'If of Protestantism in Dundee, the home of D. C. Thomson & Co.

If anyone has heard of this fortress into which no stranger may pass, not for long anyway, it is in connection with the unlikely conflagration of comics that has been pouring out of it for forty years — the picture comics *Beano* and *Dandy*, the story comics *Hotspur*, *Wizard* and *Adventure*. The backbone of these periodicals was the talent of Dudley D. Watkins. Through year upon year Watkins drew Desperate Dan, Jimmy's Magic Patch, Our Gang, Lord Snooty and his Pals, Oor Wullie, and the Broons every week with unflagging skill. His nearest equal was George Wakefield who drew practically the whole of *Film Fun*. The Broons, over the years, provide a perfect picture of the sort of people Thomson House caters for. Paw Broon is a merry little labourer who, for some reason, looks like a docker. He has the word 'Piece' written on his snap tin. He wears a wide, flat hat like his heavily bearded father, Gran'paw Broon, and the same dark three-piece suit. But Paw Broon wears a tie, probably with a tiepin fastening the two points of the collar together *underneath* the knot, whilst Gran'paw wears a muffler knotted tightly round and round his neck like a kerchief. Paw takes his cap off in the house to reveal his bald skull. Gran'paw is never seen without his cap. He probably sleeps in it. Despite the darkness of the two strands of hair plastered across his bald patch Paw Broon has a white walrus moustache of some grandeur into which he stuffs his malodorous pipe. He has no use for cufflinks. His sleeves are always rolled, even under his coat.

Maw Broon is a smiling bright-eyed giantess, proprietorial, somewhat genteel, devoid of sentiment or sensuality, full of brusque Scottish common sense and sharp good nature. Despite the neatness of her attire and the severity with which her hair is drawn back into a bun, she has borne her jovial sire eight children.

Maggie Broon is a smasher, given to somewhat unwanted vanity, but bright and decent. If she were saucy she would be like one of Donald McGill's postcard girls, but although she gets the men and indeed adores the flattery of their attention, she is unlikely to provide anything beyond a goodnight kiss. She is never seen on the sofa, up the alley, in the back seat, or in the shrubberies, those classic breeding grounds of the comically libidinous. Her brother Hen is a lofty idiot with a short back-and-sides and a suit that looks half a size too small. Her sister, Daphne Broon (bless her), is plain and lumpen, more hardworking and deserving than Maggie and often, in the hand of fate, rewarded above Maggie as befits her more modest character and as a consolation for her appearance.

Joe Broon is the tough brother with fair crew-cut hair and a jutting jaw. He is a boxer and a footballer and sometimes brings friends indoors who look as though they might not be the sort of person the family usually mixes with — Catholics perhaps. Horace Broon is a bespectacled, knobbly-kneed schoolboy, studious, level-headed, expected to go far. A swot. The Broon Twins are younger versions of Oor Wullie, crop-headed lobby-urchins grinning at the edge of family dramas. The Bairn is a dire, curly-haired brat, impulsive and eccentric, inclined to idealise and copy her pretty elder sister.

They live in a tenement in a shabby Glasgow street with a dado on the landing and all down the stone stairs. Their tenement is warm and clean and simply furnished. There are only two easy chairs, so most of the time the family sit around on hard chairs. They spend most evenings at home and would argue terribly were it not for the pacifying good nature of Maw and Paw. The television doesn't feature very largely in their lives. None of the family drinks, not even Paw when he goes out to join his mates for a game of dominoes.

So there they are, the backbone of the working class. Typical of those thousands of scrubbed industrious families who can live in the middle of the most vicious slum in Europe happily and gratefully, keeping themselves to themselves, the sideboards polished and the landing scrubbed, impervious to the cultural brew that is the main subject of this book; or seemingly impervious, until one sees that the very arch optimism by which they ignore their pungent environment has a tone to it that is a fine, sickly lavender note of sheer vulgarity.

The Broons are always heralded in by a little rhyme at the top of the page: 'In comes Paw and only then — does Maw see what's wrong with Hen' — 'Troubled with an ankle sprain? — Here's how *not* to cure the pain.' The tone of these little homilies is precisely the clue to the loophole whereby the common denominators of body and punishing hard work reassert themselves. By their sheer common sense the Broons render themselves poignantly naked, and so do the editors of the *Sunday Post*, a sort of Scottish regional *Weekly News* in which the Broons appear.

The voice is that querulous Scottish incantation laden with fair-mindedness, objectivity and self-righteousness — the voice of a tenement Fyffe Robertson. Imagine such a voice transforming, and therefore unintentionally underlining, the viciousness in this particularly choice bit of Glasgow life:

### THE THUG MADE A BIG MISTAKE WHEN HE PICKED ON THIS PRETTY GIRL

Sybil Verner, a 17-year-old machinist, lives in Dalmarnock, Glasgow.

Recently she was at a dance with her brother and three other couples.

They were preparing to leave when a burly lout, bent on trouble,

grabbed one of the lads by the lapels and hurled him over a table.

Onlookers gasped as Sybil, cool as you please, faced up to the thug.

In James Bond style she gave him a karate kick on the knee.

As he doubled in pain, she floored him with two vicious chops on the back of the neck.

The thug's mates couldn't believe their eyes.

How could a slip of a girl k.o. one of them?

They waited outside the hall for Sybil and her friends.

Another so-called tough-nut barred their way, challenging them all to a fight.

Again Sybil stepped forward. Wham! Bang! Pow!

She knocked him cold with two karate punches to the jaw and a neck chop.

The rest of the hard men quietly slipped away.

What they hadn't appreciated is Sybil's a Brown Belt expert in karate.

That's one step below being a Black Belt.

When she was 14 she was attacked by a gang of girls.

She was badly beaten. Her nose was broken.

She determined it would never happen again.

She joined the Kobe Osaka Karate Club.

Now she can smash her hand through a slate.

She's scared of no-one — as two Glasgow thugs painfully know!

The centre-page stories, more incredible than even those of the *Weekly News*, all have this cheery baldness and these matter-of-fact Hemingwayesque paragraphs. Mrs Sadie Crawford, 128, Thornhill Rd, Falkirk, has a nasty time with a pet piranha. 'The little blighter left a half-inch gash.' 'George's Fitba' Boots Have To Be Kept In Police Custody' we are informed with a nod in the direction of the dialect, whilst 'Two Years Of Torment For Glasgow Girl', a tale of an unfortunate child who was bitten by radioactive gnats, finishes, 'Little did her parents know that a midge attack would be the start of years of torment.'

But the Doc, who replies to queries and complaints in the medical advice column, is the man whose unsparing Calvinistic zeal and jaunty bedside manner will lead us past the political forum where we are told 'The answer is ENOCH' and where some sardonic Machiavelli inquires, 'Is there a busier little bee than Bernadette?' — past the editorial orators who exhorted the miners to return to work: 'You know it's for the best, lads' — past the rhetorician who asked of Whitelaw, 'Can Willie handle the hot potato?' — past the Sheriff of Dundee as he shrieks to the Scottish Council of Women Citizens for 'tough prisons which make life hell for the inmates' — and on, through the litter of old rags and dancing tattered newspapers, kicking tin cans under the gaping sockets of the shattered ground-floor windows of the Gorbals, to the sparsely furnished back kitchen where a man sits who has 'very dry hands and the skin keeps cracking, mostly at the finger and thumb'. 'A fungus,' cries the Doc and leaves ointment. On we trudge through the Clydeside fog to the wild-eyed solitary who tells us, 'I have a nodule on top of my left ear.' 'Yes,' says the Doc. 'It's probably just a simple thing but all unusual lumps should be checked.'

Women await us in the alley outside. 'My husband,' croaks one, 'My husband (75) has developed a trembling in his arm. Is it his heart?' Before she has finished, a second woman leans over her shoulder. 'My little girl (6½) has sticking out ears. I am letting her hair grow but you can still see them.'

'I've started to go black and blue every time I have a bath,' grates a voice from the archway. A face looms in from the left with heavy-veined lids: 'I see flashing lights, usually a circular hoop, when I close my eyes in the dark and rotate them. . . .' 'I've a small swelling under my armpit. . . . It disappears when I raise my arm above my head. . . .' A figure is beckoning us away. I follow the Doc's bouncy industrious figure. The voices fade behind us and through the dim-lit twilight we can see a pale face, and a clerical collar below it. The voice is confidential and urgent: 'I'm a minister of 57 who can't get out of the habit of running up stairs two at a time' — suddenly, before the Doc has had a chance to offer his remedy, the Godly man is off like a Jack-o'-lantern up the alley-stairs. From the distance comes the sound of tinkling glass as Sybil Verner throws another thug through a window.

# COMPETITORS

The circus has failed because it has lost the basis of its appeal. The few large circuses that remain have the well-polished, self-conscious look of museum artifacts, the patina of a carefully preserved identity. It has attempted to create the myth of wonder, as though its audiences were children sharing in a lost past. In the high summer of its time the audience for the circus was an adult one. The adult world no longer finds in the circus a microcosm of the wonderment of the great natural world, of an idyll in which men and beasts perform together in uneasy truce. The whip of the ringmaster cracks with a more sinister sound, the lions' flanks are rubbed smooth like the hide of a totter's pony chafed by imprisoning shafts. They bear the scars of their servitude as do the 'artistes'. They perform for 'your wonder and amazement' tricks that a junior school tyro gymnast would disdain. But unlike the gymnast, they are relieved from competition. As one watches the gymnasts perform in the Olympics one is aware that they are striving for dominance over their rival competitors. So evenly matched are they that we seek other qualities than technical skill, a quality of expression which denies man's physical limitations, that strives to assert that 'Homo athleticus' is True Man. We all become Audience, united in our inadequacy. We are presented with the conundrum, that the Natural world possesses a grace and beauty, a skilfulness and speed of limb and eye, *naturally*. We must strive to recall it. The trapezists

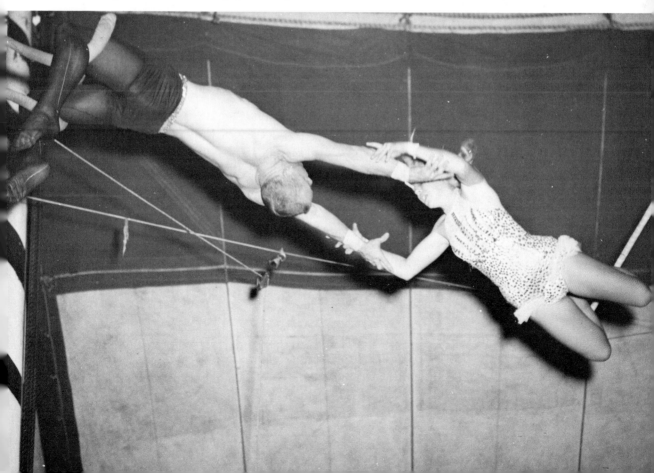

have no such intention to appear in an athletic role. Theirs is a natural skill. They must swing and fall and catch and fly as effortlessly as a riveter catches his red-hot piece of metal or the potter's fingers apply the exact pressure, with all the practised ease of journeymen. They do not attempt to emulate the supernatural powers of demigods. They are contained, practised and safe. They present an illusion of gods, dressed in vaguely allegorical costumes, spangled and glittered, with cloaks to hide their divinity when they walk on the same level as mortals, to be cast aside as they clamber, with displays of enormous effort, up rope ladders, demonstrating the dragging force of the earth as their muscles strain in their forearms — they must not use their legs like sensible men. Unlike the gymnast they perform in the dark, for it is an entertainment which casts the audience in the role of voyeur at an act of possible self-destruction. The danger suggested by rolls of drums, requests for silence, and flashing beams of dazzling light.

In the few small travelling shows which still tour this country, the audience is united in pathetic anguish as the tatty and impoverished performers sketch out the

lineaments of a dead culture. They are so incompetent, so lacking in the glitter and hard gloss of showbiz, that the audience is caught up in a conspiracy of sympathy and admiration for the sheer ordinariness of the actors. They identify with the lady who tries to pull her plump body on to a swing, feel for her puffing efforts and pretend at the interval not to recognise her when she tends the candy-floss machine. The sparseness of the audience deprives the individual of the anonymity of the group and forces him into a more intimate part, like a game of charades. On one occasion, during the performance of the strong-man act of the famous Circus Marcus, it was necessary to invite the participation of some members of the audience to climb on to a plank held in the air by the self-styled Hercules. Because the audience was so small his full power could not be amply tested as he insisted that one lady remain seated to constitute an audience. Someone must remain detached to express 'amazement and wonder' while he lifted the rest of the audience above the ground.

In the Olympic arena commentators constantly emphasise the mental strain of competition. Athletes 'sweat it out', suffer agonies of suspense; the battle is within, a struggle against the athlete's weaker nature. The whole of mankind is involved, world records are shattered, objects are hurled further than ever before by any human hand, the human body is lifted off the ground to ever greater heights, dashes between two points in a shorter time. A new concept of time is evoked. Records are broken in 'shattering' and 'unbelievable' split seconds, measured by the most complex electronic equipment. Fractions of time that human eye and brain are incapable of perceiving assume a significance of grotesque importance — the difference between being a loser and a winner. The winner is the only competitor who achieves fulfilment, who has passed all the tests, who has made the greatest sacrifice, the greatest demands on his body, the one who is proved to be the possessor of the greatest gifts. This implication of a religious experience can only explain the seriousness of the competitors, their emphasis on the initiatory role of their preparation, their faith in the transcending nature of the otherwise meaningless and futile activities. These are denials rather than deeds, deprivations rather than attainments. They no longer speak of fitness but of competitive spirit, of pain barriers, of that single-mindedness that moves the mind to another plane of existence. That St Bernard's holiness was expressed by his lack of awareness of whether he drank wine or vinegar, reduced his earthly existence to insignificance, his body a despicable mortality to be abused and despised. The paradox of the athlete is that his paradise is of this world, the rewards all too material for an activity which he produces in bursts rather than as a sustained way of life. For only winning can bring relief from the struggle to succeed. The Olympic competitor is not an entertainer. His deeds only achieve heroic proportions when he defeats his fellows. No matter how great the struggle of the loser, his efforts remain untransformed and meaningless in the shame of his failure.

# SPORT

It was made abundantly clear, in a recent survey of the social and domestic life of a group of English professional footballers, that the game still represents one of the ways whereby a boy with little beyond basic secondary education, a working-class boy, can elevate himself in a material sense without causing a radical change in his class values. Moving up the social ladder usually involves the whole complex alteration of a life-style, different viewpoints, different standards and rewards, different habits, clothes and activities. The brief, highly rewarded life of a footballer insulates him from the social group whose earning power is equal to his. With the Professions, medicine, the law, accountancy or dentistry, or Business, earning is a means of acquiring a good house, a car and of course clothes.

Sports wear is the major influence on clothes in the last twenty years. The footballer, however, is a member of a team and so must wear a distinguishing uniform, shorts and a club strip. Off the field he will tend towards a dignified appearance, modish and 'smart' with cuff-links and cravats, a play-boy rather than an off-duty player. His clothes contrast with his working garb — not for him the emblematic stripes and numbers. He emphasises his freedom and independence. Certainly, in spite of efforts from the menswear trade, short pants have not become fashionable with men as everyday wear. Men's legs look well with bare feet on a beach, but the boy-scout, sunburnt-knee image dies hard.

Golf, not being a team game, allows its practitioners to command the tournament field with ease. In contest, the Pros stroll freely over the shaved lawns and pleasant fairways of the course, walking constantly, pausing only to propel the ball before them. The crowd of spectators flutters and regroups, giving shape to the match. The players are indistinguishable from the spectators, with whom they share a common interest in the game as *participants*. Gone are the flat caps and baggy plus-fours of the thirties and forties. There is no longer a golf suit, but simple loose jerseys to allow unrestricted movement, narrow, well-creased trousers, and specialised shoes to grip the ground.

The crowd as they gather round the green at Muirfield wait as Jacklin or Trevino, Palmer or Nicklaus, play up to the flag. We see the tiny figures in the distance, only distinguishable from the crowd by the cleared space around them, a glint of light on the shaft of the club, a sight of the whiteness of the ball against the blue glare of the sky before it plops and rolls. It rolls up to my foot, so close I can easily read the message on it without stopping — Penfold and a number. Doug Sanders, who has struck it there, strolls up and joins in our contemplation. 'Son of a bitch.' He addresses my companion, Peter Stit, with the ease and familiarity of an old friend in adversity. Indeed they are indistinguishable in dress — jerseys and slacks and bare-headed. 'What ya think?' 'I think it's straight.' He is like a general planning his strategy with his trusted advisers. Peter, who knows the course, makes a contemplative noise. Sanders waits with us while his partner plays his shot. He is part of the audience. Then he steps forward and strikes the ball straight at the hole. It rolls away from us and disappears into the ground. Sanders straightens, hands his club to his caddy, nods in appreciation to Peter and strolls off to the next tee. 'Christ,' says Peter. 'That's the best putt I've played.' These professional golfers are amongst the best-known men in the world. They make enormous amounts of money — playing. Yet for them there is no distance between them and the audience. They exchange roles and identities with consummate ease. Here are no mounted police, no crush barriers. The crowd are controlled by themselves. They stand patiently on one side of a piece of string. Many spectators are dressed for a game of golf and only lack the clubs. The Pros play the shots for them. They have their left hands encased in a driving glove and a Mister Lu straw hat on their head, and one feels that at any moment any one of the audience will detach himself and, stepping forward, will stroke the ball with delicacy of touch down the fairway and into the cup and then, with modest smile, step back into the audience and applaud the next player. The pro golfer differs radically from the pro footballer in his response to the public. The golfer finds in his work a social integration with society — the footballer is deprived. He hates and despises the people who squirm and seeth on the terraces. If he is not afraid of them he is a fool. He needs the assistance of the police to do his job, and very little appreciation or respect is paid to his skills. Like a pop star he is distanced from the audience, tarted up in clownish stripes, with mudded knees and constant agitation. Off the park he must invent an identity for himself which further distances him.

The golfer strolls, the footballer spurts. He is an athlete, the golfer is fit. Tied to his place of work, like a mill-hand, the golfer roams the world. No scandal attaches to the golfer; if he wishes to drink in night-clubs all night, no press man thinks it worthy of comment. Contact with the real world destroys the footballer.

The road forks four ways. One way leads to Bradford, one to Halifax, one to Huddersfield, and one to Leeds. The far horizon is the topmost Pennine ridge beyond which lie Manchester and Liverpool. All around are moors. Between the road junction and the moors there is a moon landscape of industrial waste. Majestic hills and valleys are scarred, pitted, shaved bare, scored, poisoned. Massive stone edifices and monuments built to last for ever are starkly empty, crumbling. The landscape smokes like a scene of recent disaster from which the fumes are still drifting. Banks of freshly dropped slag are hot underfoot. Railway embankments and abandoned tramways of slag dropped a hundred years ago crack open and emit the smells, the tar smells, the coal-gas smells, the spread sewerage of the nineteenth century.

Between the Bradford Road and the Halifax Road there is a chapel. Written crudely on the black stone is the simple creed: WE PREACH CHRIST CRUCIFIED.

Between the Halifax Road and the Huddersfield Road is a public shithouse. A bus shelter divides the sexes. The heavy porcelain of these conveniences was shattered long ago but people still squat over the jagged edges. One complete bowl has been dragged out and left, half keeled-over on the pavement, the shit still hanging from its earth pipe and the cistern pipe dragging behind it like a rusty umbilical cord. The bus shelter is a richly layered tablet of hieroglyphics. Aerosol lies across felt-tip pen, felt-tip pen lies across wax crayon, wax crayon lies across Biro and Biro lies across graphite. Knife and chisel score across the lot. Shelf Rockers, Buttershaw Skins, Tong Suedes, Low Moor Grebos, Daz, Baz, Jaz, and Leeds United rule, OK.

Between the Bradford Road and the Leeds Road lies a pub. Its exterior is solid stone with iron railings and massive area walls. Steep stone steps lead into a flashy plastic interior. The doors have upholstered panels of black leather with tiny buttons. At the bar you lean on a long plastic cushion as you sink your straight glass of bitter Tetley's mild.

On Sunday lunchtimes the pub regulars are present *en masse*. They are young labourers with loud local accents, T-shirts, denims or the trousers of Italian suits, buckled tightly across packed buttocks. Their hair, and the remnants on brown knuckles and forearms of self-administered tattoos, bear witness to their having belonged in their teens to one or another of the fashionable tribes who advertise themselves on the bus-shelter wall across the roundabout. They are talking about a trip to a football match the previous afternoon. The coach, it seems, was wrecked. Urine and beer ran so freely in the aisle that the driver stopped and refused to go on until his vehicle was cleaned. Several of the passengers were mechanics and drivers. They thrust him aside and drove themselves home. One of them is present and he tells the story with great hilarity. The contrast between this boasted violence and vandalism, and the polished luxury in which it is re-counted, points out the special nature of the violence. This is no Irishman's vomitorium where each Saturday a sheet of hardboard replaces yet another pane of glass. These are no alcoholics although they are all capable boozers with a ten-pint-a-day average intake. They have separated themselves from the juvenile groups in which they first smashed street lamps and terrorised the aged. Their violence is partisan. This pub is their home. Their barracks. Foreign territory is fair game. When visiting foreign territory the signature must be left. Members of the opposite clan will recognise this exchange of insignia. Only the city fathers will condemn it morally, and who gives a fuck about them?

While they were on the coach the previous afternoon, swilling ale, not

so seriously involved in football as they are in the sport to which they have graduated, their younger brothers and cousins were foregathering in Bradford pedestrian precinct so that they could, in vast numbers, descend on Exchange Station and commandeer a Leeds train to go to Elland Road and support the Kings of the North.

These are the groups who broke away from the American-orientated pop fashions in 1968 and espoused a fashion which was a caricature of working gear — baggy jeans with braces, white shirts with rolled-up sleeves, Doc Martin boots and shaven heads. They were the skinheads and they celebrated a return to a British working-class identity by emulating their labourer brothers' labouring clothes. Since then their fashions have changed rapidly through the Crombie overcoats and trilbies copied from West Indians and street-market gangsters, through calf-length dungarees, long hair once more, in emulation of George Best and Charlie George, and black, studded army boots, on through the uniform of foot-wide tartan bags, high-collar shirts and peaked caps with bobbles on the crown, on to the current arrays of wool caps and wrist scarves. Many of them are armed with a formidable array of weapons, bread knives, meat skewers, hatchets, all of them more vicious than the flick knife and bicycle chain of their teddy-boy fathers. Before they embark the police, gathering already, will herd them out of the precinct and they will spread throughout the town, roaring through the markets towards the station, tipping up goods, knocking off hats and chanting the name of their hero.

Four weeks ago their Manchester counterparts wrecked the shopping centre of Halifax. Last week, in a battle of flung stones and bottles in Leeds, they shattered bus windows, badly scarring respectable citizens. Paris trembles in recollection. They are the crude first flowering of a need to shatter the confining structures of class and neighbourhood without betraying class loyalty. They use the football team as royal representatives of the community, beyond reproach and therefore granting the same licence to their armed supporters. Thus the supporters can give full vent to that frustration built up in the carefully streamed school, in the closely knit family, in the closely knit neighbourhood. They can give vent to the most outrageous violence. Release is claimed by upholding the *idea* of the community, thus escaping the *actual* community without betraying it.

On the whole civic bodies recognise this. Few football fans are manhandled in the cells the way hippies were. No football ground will be closed the way UFO and Middle Earth were. No football teams will be harassed the way the Rolling Stones were, simply because they all bear the name of a community and represent the community *as a whole*, and not a dissident breakaway group.

But that was all yesterday and now it is Sunday lunchtime in a pub set between

the road to Leeds and the road to Bradford, and the older brothers are finishing their last pint of the lunchtime session before they file out and over the road to support, or maybe play for, Bradford Northern Rugby League team. This graduation from soccer to rugby is a graduation from the ostentatious violence of the skinhead for a sport which is scarcely violent at all, to a ritual that is a weekly celebration of smashed teeth and broken ribs. Only last week Northern and Warrington, a Lancashire team whose numbers include the incendiary Murphy, obeyed the old supporter's cry of, 'Ne'er 'eed t' ball, gerron wi't' game.' Supporters swarmed across the pitch to back up their knight errants and continued the onslaught with bricks and bottles outside the ground afterwards.

Odsal Stadium, the old home of Bradford Northern, is set between the Leeds Road and the Huddersfield Road. A vast natural crater on the crown of the hill, helped along with many tons of slag, cinders, clay, compressed refuse, this distinguished amphitheatre has, from the road, all the majesty of a boarded-in building-site. Walled by a rich collage of waste timber whose faded colours have at some time advertised Webster's Perfect Ales, it is entered by one tiny turnstile. Once through the gate, what remains of Yorkshire stretches away to the hills beyond the pitch. Once down the precipitous bank to the wooden barriers enclosing the ground itself, everything disappears from view but the grandstand, a gaunt resonant barn, the Member's Club with its Stage Four club room and bar, a shithouse that looks like an air-raid shelter whose painted bricks still advertise the show-jumping events of 1956, and two hot-dog stands that glitter like tarts at a funeral. Shortly it is to be transformed. An underpass will replace the crossroads and an Olympic fantasy will rival this familiar battered arena.

In the long summer evenings, as the nostalgic rays of the late sun wash down from Pennistone and Slaithwaite, it is magical to see this desolate hilltop suddenly animated with small knots of people hurrying to the support of the summer

Bradford Northern team. In summer, Bradford Northern means speedway.

This is a different crowd from the young stalwarts who go to rugby or the young psychopaths who go to soccer, although a small group of yobos circles the top of the arena bank, ignoring the sport, eyeing one another. This is a family crowd. Whole groups are bunched hurriedly together in identical scarves or supporters' T-shirts. Over the whole crowd is that curious sense that this is that element in the working class that has a morbid fascination for the mechanical and a complete lack of interest in home-building. The windcheaters and sporty badges and drab ex-military gear have overtones of those not-so-distant days when cycling and the rejuvenation of worn-out car and cycle engines was one of the few pastimes, together with the breeding of whippets and pigeons, that the working class could easily afford. And here and there an ear-ring or a knuckle tattoo betrays an ex-rocker. Sometimes there are hordes of rockers, not the recently fashionable Hell's Angels copyists but ageing young men in worn black leather with silver studs, long greasy hair and filthy faces, riding Triumphs and Nortons. To a degree this is a celebration of the internal combustion engine in its simplest stripped-down form. These are no boozers, no community partisans. They make little noise. Their demeanour is the opposite of the swaying, roaring exaltation of a football crowd. They concentrate hard. They carry scoreboards with bulldog clips which they study absorbedly before the contest begins. They are utterly dedicated. Fanatics. To what they are really dedicated is disturbingly evident as the evening goes on.

The loudspeaker belts out the charts. Suddenly it stops. The music switches to a brisk march. The announcer announces the teams. Up till now one or two riders have been idly tooling their machines round the track, which is banked slightly and composed of loose red shale. Now, led by four titty little cheer-leaders in rather grubby uniforms, the two teams walk out to take their places behind their bikes which are lined up before the grandstand.

The music stops and each rider is introduced. As he is introduced he steps forward and mounts his machine. These are hard, tough, scruffy young men. They are probably what every greaser really always wanted to be. They have the same rough edges, but skill and the most insane daring replace the rocker's destructive exhibitionism. The uniforms, padded leather suits with colours worn overtop in the form of plastic jackets, visor-like crash helmets with jaw-pieces, tattered throat rags which are later worn over the face like a cowboy's neckerchief against fumes and flying cinders, are heraldic in colouring but clouded with layers of dirt.

Each team circles the arena, reaping its applause. The visiting team is the Boston Barracudas. They get little applause. Bradford Northern carry their eight-

year-old mascots on the tanks of the leading bikes. Their applause is thunderous but brief. The bikes sing waspishly. The fumes filling the air have the slightly alarming smell of an overheated chip-pan. All the riders disappear into the pits.

The first race is announced. Four riders, two from each team, are pushed off. These bikes have neither starting mechanisms nor brakes. Attendants in white coats and blue caps shove them off, they circle the track once and come into line at the starting post before the grandstand. The noise and fumes of their engines fill the stand and the ramshackle old structure amplifies the roar with its scarred boards and galvanised roof until it resonates like some demonic organ.

The referee is a man who looks in his white coat like a secondary-school woodwork master. It seems odd to see him hold such easy control over a pack of dusty roughnecks. He checks the line-up and suddenly ducks and runs between the bikes so that he is behind them. At the same moment the wire clicks up and the race is on.

The race is uninterrupted, formalised lunacy. Engines and fuel, a fuel called dope and reputedly composed of oil and pure alcohol, intended for the open skies, are being used in a space comparatively like a back lawn. The first bend is taken at a skid, the bike levels up for a few yards and then the other end of the track demands another sideways two-wheel drift. Each race involves four trips round the track. By the second trip sheer centrifugal force has driven every bike within a yard of the barrier. Each time they hurtle past the grandstand the roof and the board receive the sound like some vast echoing mouth. Overtaking is virtually impossible. If it happens it is called a takeover and is as much an accident as anything else. By the third trip the leading bikes have no chance to straighten out of their skids and are forced to circle the track wildly, broadside on, like two balls on string being spun in space at a frantic speed. The noise, the danger and the violence are so great the crowd is stunned to a maniacal silence. As they stand on their seats calmly drinking in the madness the waves of sound rise from the ground, from the boards, up their limbs to their very genitals. A rain of flung gravel spatters their impervious faces.

Crewe has a rider called Phil Crump who is renowned for his recklessness but tonight one of the Bradford riders is content to hurtle round the track on a bike completely out of control. Wobbling like a haptic snake, its roar revved up to a scream, the bike leaves the other riders behind time and again, spurting back shale so that the mere mortals in the wake terminate the race caked blind from head to foot. It looks as though it is being ridden by a dummy and is virtually driving itself.

Control by the abandonment of control. Absolute triumph by absolute withdrawal. Madness, a single stripped-down bike hurtling crazily round the track and leaving all behind it in a shower of filth. The rider is Robin Adlington. In the fourth race he attempts a takeover and crashes straight into the side of a Boston rider. A gasp leaves the mouth of a Boston supporter, like a ghostly bird. A god has permitted himself to be brought down. God or not, the Barracuda is a tumble artist. Balled up like a hedgehog, he rolls over several times, stands up and walks off. The crowd clap him politely. They seem oddly disappointed. At the point of the disaster spectators came rushing down to the barrier to see the details. They climbed back to their places with a slightly disconsolate air.

The next crash occurs two races later. A rider is shaken loose from his bike on a corner and hits the barrier, which expands and springs together again as though mounted on elastic. The siren stops the race. The stretcher is rushed out. The boy, his back arched, his face contorted with pain, is carried past the stand to the pits. A roar of applause rises and it seems that for the first time old-fashioned sportsmanship is being demonstrated at Odsal. And indeed that is the guise under which the applause is permitted, but if you listen carefully to the slightly hysterical edge on the applause, sportsmanship is not the whole nature of the applause by any means. The crowd has come for violence. They are not just clapping the brave rider. They are clapping the first blood.

And back we are drawn beyond those streets through which the *Sunday Post*

Doc might lead us to those dark and muscular domestic hells where repression concentrates the energies into a thirst for physicality and revenge. Back we drift into the musky bedroom where kids like angels sprawl in wet sheets just beyond the hanging blanket. Elephant mounds are stirring through the weight of beer and spuds; genitals are lifting and lubricating through the mud of fear and shame and bitterness and grey fatigue. The single bulb hanging on its tattered flex from a cracked ceiling is an overhead floodlight. The referee in his white shirt, with his bow tie, is at the bedside. Mick McManus and Jackie Pallo, Klondike Bill and Vic Feather, successions of fleshed and sweating villains, are joined in malodorous congress. Faces are squeezed like sponges in grappling clumsy hands, are wrenched in unexpected ecstasies of pain and exertion. Knackers hang in their soiled sacks between thighs that bear a wire mesh of fuzz. A head is wrenched to a pitch of purple by a heaving crotch. Gargantua is giving birth to Pantagruel. Buttocks and biceps rise like ancient fish in light and cigarette smoke. Mother bites her lip, grandmother rubs her knees in anxiety, daughter leaps in uncontrolled electric spasms. The devil is joined with the devil on the mattress in the single bedroom. The falsehoods are stripped away. Our fears are naked, formalised and distanced, guyed and celebrated, locked in combat for our survival and renewal. The nocturnal gymnasium echoes: 'Kill him! Kill the bastard!'